TWO MIDDLE-A
IN ANDALUSIA

Penelope Chetwode is the daughter of a Field Marshal who spent her early years in India. Her husband was Sir John Betjeman. She is also the living definition of a certain kind of intrepid English-woman.

'Miss Chetwode has an extraordinary gift for interesting one in everything she does, says or thinks.' *The Sunday Times*

That gift is expressed to the full in *Two Middle-Aged Ladies in Andalusia*, which the author first penned in 1963 as a record of her Spanish riding tour undertaken in the previous year. The other 'middle-aged lady', and her companion on the road, was her mare *La Marquesa*. In best Cervantean tradition, rider and mount set out with a generous amount of spirit and daring, not dampened by the fact that they possess but a minimal knowledge of the language. This book recreates both the rigours and the rewards experienced and enjoyed en route. The author seeks out the remotest parts of the countryside, and some of the primitive rural inns she visits have changed little since the days when they used to house the nineteenth century travel writers – such as George Borrow and Richard Ford – who inspired her journey.

The unworldly beauty of the Andalusian children; the troglodyte colony; the beautiful Grimms-fairy-tale village of Tiscar: these are all to be savoured as well as the satisfaction of 'seeing human beings as God made them to be'. The reader of *Two Middle-Aged Ladies in Andalusia* rides in tandem with one of the most lively and candid of travellers – always fascinated by animals, human nature, food, sanitation and architecture – through the less accessible regions of Spain.

Penelope Chetwode lives in Hay-on-Wye in Hereford.

The cover shows a painting of Seville by Myles Birkett Foster by kind permission of the Townley Hall Art Gallery and Museums, Burnley

Two
Middle-Aged Ladies
in Andalusia

PENELOPE CHETWODE

CENTURY
LONDON MELBOURNE AUCKLAND JOHANNESBURG

To Amber L'Estrange
to whom I owe an eternal debt

First published in 1963 by John Murray (Publishers) Ltd

© Penelope Chetwode 1963

This edition first published in 1985
by Century Publishing Co. Ltd
Second impression 1986 by Century,
an imprint of Century Hutchinson Ltd,
Brookmount House, 62–65 Chandos Place, London WC2N 4NN

Century Hutchinson Publishing Group (Australia) Pty Ltd,
PO Box 496, 16–22 Church Street, Hawthorn,
Melbourne, Victoria 3122

Century Hutchinson Group (NZ) Ltd,
PO Box 40–086, 32–34 View Road, Glenfield, Auckland 10

Century Hutchinson Group (SA) Pty Ltd,
PO Box 337, Berglvei 2012, South Africa

ISBN 0 7126 0462 6

ACKNOWLEDGEMENTS

My thanks are due first and foremost to the Duke of Wellington for providing me with my companion, the other middle-aged lady; then to Bill and Annie Davis for a thousand kindnesses and above all for selecting such an exciting district for us to explore; to Eudo and Rosemary Tonsen-Rye for invaluable help and advice; to Don Antonio Navarrete, Mayor of Quesada, for permission to publish his poem on page 81 and to Gamel Woolsey for her superb translation of it; to my husband John Betjeman and my friend Patsy Ward for pestering me relentlessly to overcome my natural sloth and edit my diaries to produce this book; to another old and loyal friend, Karen Lancaster, for tireless work on the typescript and proofs; and last of all to the Reverend Mother Abbess and the community at Goodings Convent for providing the perfect atmosphere in which to write.

In quoting the spoken word I have followed the colloquial custom in Andalusia of clipping the final consonants.

GOODINGS. FEAST OF ST MARK 1963

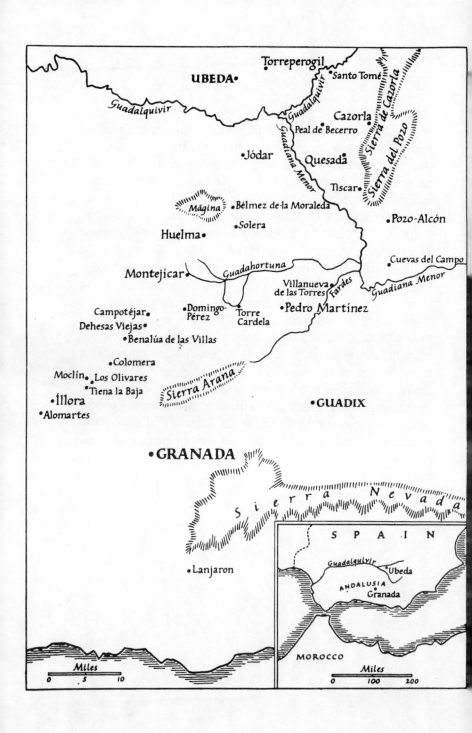

IT WAS THE HORSE that brought me to Spain. For years enthusiastic friends had tried in vain to make me go there. I pointed out that two countries, Italy and India, were enough for ten lifetimes. How, in middle age, could I be expected to mug up the history, language and architecture of a country about which I knew next to nothing? I had not even read a line of *Don Quixote*. I knew Italian fairly well and if I now tried to learn Spanish I should inevitably confuse the two and end by speaking neither. I dug in my toes and obstinately refused to be lured to the peninsula by ardent hispanophils.

Then, in a Sunday paper, I read about conducted riding tours in Andalusia. My resistance suddenly broke down and I booked to go in late October.

St Thomas says you cannot love a horse because it cannot love you back.* This statement proved a serious obstacle to my entering the Holy Roman Church in 1948. Then Evelyn Waugh pointed out that St Thomas was an Italian accustomed to seeing his father's old chargers sent along to the local salami factory in Aquino. Had he been an English theologian he would never have written like that: his father's chargers would have been pensioned off in the park. Now I was going to a Latin country where old horses ended their lives in the bull-ring. Could I stand such an attitude to animals? I who had always been full of the traditional English sentimentality towards them? This racial antipathy was well illustrated some years ago when I brought my daughter's pony into the kitchen and kissed it in front of Gina, our Calabrian maid: 'In Italia bacciamo uomini!' (In Italy we kiss men) she had said in utter scorn.

*   *   *

When I first arrived at Alora, the starting-point of the

* St Thomas Aquinas: *Summa Theologica*, 11a, 11ae, Q. 23, article 1.

conducted tour, and saw the wiry little horses of the sierras, I got rather a shock. Standing between fourteen and fifteen hands high they were so much narrower than our own mountain and moorland breeds, and their conformation was decidedly odd: they had ewe necks, cow hocks and unusually straight pasterns. Nevertheless they turned out to be extremely fit, and were surprisingly good rides. They walked out well, never stumbled down the stoniest mountain paths, and had armchair canters. The soles of their feet must have been an inch thick as they never bruised them on the roughest going nor went lame from any other cause. Their narrowness would have been tiring on long rides but the Andalusian saddles provided the width which the animals lacked. They were high fore and aft, had soft sheepskin seats and were almost impossible to fall out of. Beautifully embroidered leather *alforjas* (saddle-bags) were hung over the cantles at the back and it was astounding what a lot one could cram into them.

The feeding of horses in southern Spain is extremely interesting because it is so different from our own. They get neither oats nor hay but *paja y cebada*, which is chopped barley straw chaff and barley corn fed dry. According to Richard Ford* 8 lb barley is equal in feeding value to 10 lb oats because it contains less husk. The manger is first filled with straw chaff then the corn is mixed well into it. In the morning, before giving the first feed, any chaff that remains and any dust in the manger are scooped out onto the floor to form the deep litter on which the animals are bedded. In the *posada* stables this is a muck mystic's dream, with the droppings of horses, mules, donkeys, pigs, goats, hens and human

---

* Richard Ford: *Gatherings from Spain*, ch. VIII (John Murray). Richard Ford (1796–1858) travelled in Spain from 1830 to 1833. His *Handbook for Travellers in Spain* was published by John Murray in 1845. *Gatherings from Spain* was published in 1846: it appeared later in the Everyman Library but is now out of print.

beings perfectly composted with chopped barley straw, wood ash, onion and other vegetable peelings. It is sweet-smelling, as all the best deep litter should be; nor did I ever notice any sign of thrush in the animal's feet. Greenmeat is provided by lucerne cut and fed in the manger, or by grass when it can be found by people with no land of their own on which to grow lucerne. The animals are also taken out to graze when work and time allow, usually along streams or irrigation canals where there is always a bit of grass, or up on the mountains where there are several plants which are eaten with great relish. When grazing they are either hobbled or put in charge of a boy. Morning and evening they are led out to water at the *fuente* (a trough sometimes fed by a spring, sometimes by piped supply) and when on a journey they are encouraged to drink at every stream they ford.

In England I would despise a conducted riding tour because English is my language and I am a one-inch map maniac and a lot of my delight lies in working out routes on my maps beforehand and in poring over them afterwards. But going to Spain for the first time with next to no Spanish and very poor maps, I decided that the best preparation for a solo ride (my avowed ambition) was to go on a preliminary one with people who knew the ropes: thus I hoped to learn about Spanish blacksmiths, feeding methods, inns, and cross-country navigation. I would also mug up a stable vocabulary.

I chose one of the cheap tours run by Antonio Llomelini Tabarca which was wonderful value for money, costing only £28 for a fortnight, full board and lodging of horse and rider included. Antonio is a young Sevillian whose chief delight has been to explore the sierras of his native Andalusia on a horse and now he has made a business of it and established an excellent riding centre in the hills at Alora, 12½ miles inland from Torremolinos.

Milking foxes

Antonio's enthusiasm, seriousness of purpose and de-lightful manners do not answer to the description given of his countrymen 120 years ago by George Borrow: 'The higher class of Andalusians are probably upon the whole the most vain and foolish of human beings with a taste for nothing but sensual amusements, foppery in dress, and ribald discourse.' *

Discourse in any case was limited by ignorance of one another's languages. On the first evening at dinner (ex-cellent *gazpacho* followed by a very good curry, his cook having spent two years with an Indian family) I attempted to talk about foxhunting. Antonio made, or rather I thought that he made, the astonishing remark that in this part of Spain vixen were milked and their milk was made into cheese. What he actually said was that poisoned cheese was put out on the hills to kill foxes. I tried to warn him against indulging in such practices when he went to work in the Cottesmore Hunt Kennels where he had arranged to go during the winter in order to learn English. Do foxes really eat cheese?

Antonio had a little rough-haired terrier on short legs, the shape of a small corgi, of which he was as fond as the most ardent English dog-lover. It always slept on his bed and was very friendly with his guests. One night I went to evening devotions in the big church across the plaza. I arrived late and fell flat across the corner of a confessional, which set a whole pew of children off into a fit of giggles. Then Chico came in, singled me out as his master's friend and came and lay down at my feet. The Blessed Sacrament was exposed and instead of letting a sleeping dog lie quite innocently in the Divine Presence I got up and carried him out. On returning to my place

---

* George Borrow: *The Bible in Spain*, Vol. III, ch. XII (John Murray). George Borrow (1803–81) travelled in Spain and Portugal as agent to The Bible Society from 1835 to 1839. His *Zincali, or The Gypsies in Spain* was published in 1841 by John Murray and *The Bible in Spain* in 1843.

4

A talented gypsy

I again fell flat over the confessional. I soon learned that it was the usual thing for dogs to wander in and out of church in Spain and that nobody minded. Many priests have dogs who regularly hear Mass sitting motionless in an aisle with apparent devotion.

The day after the fox-milking incident Antonio had to go to Seville to get his papers in order for England. Having spent a couple of days hacking through the orange groves round Alora and getting used to our saddles and horses, we set off on our ride to Ronda. Our guide was a remarkable English girl, Vicki Sumner, one of the finest types our island produces: beautiful and tough, an excellent horsewoman, she speaks fluent Andaluz and, like Ivan Petrutski Skivar, can perform on the Spanish guitar. She has a deep-rooted passion for Spain and knows the Serrania de Ronda like the inside of her pocket.

Pitirri, the gypsy groom, also came with us. He rode a pack-horse with large panniers into which we could put the overflow from our saddle-bags and the great black oilskin riding capes which formed part of our equipment. Pitirri is a man of parts; there is little he doesn't know about a horse and he acts as middleman in many a deal in and round his *pueblo*. He can also sing and dance *flamenco* with great skill and feeling. On our rides he sang endless verses in *cante jondo*, the haunting eastern type of singing in quarter tones which is common all over Andalusia. Gerald Brenan thinks it antedates the Moorish occupation and derives from a primitive type of Mediterranean music.* All I can say is that it reminded me of Indian singing with no beginning and no end: it is the music of eternity and you never get tired of it.

Besides myself there were four other clients on this tour, all of us women, and we got along splendidly. My friend Mary Clive and her daughter Alice (neither of

* Gerald Brenan: *South from Granada*, ch. x (Hamish Hamilton, 1957).

5

whom are experienced riders) rode for six-hour stretches without once complaining of fatigue; Frances Bell Mac-Donald, a professional photographer, helped me to put new films into my camera, and her friend Celia Irving carried a tape recorder for two hundred miles in her *alforjas* on which she recorded sheep bells, nightingales, Pitirri singing and hooves clattering on cobbles for a B.B.C. travel programme. The tragedy was that the musical evenings at the inns described by all the nineteenth-century travellers such as Washington Irving, Cook, Ford, Borrow and Street had now been replaced by *flamenco* music broadcast from Seville, so poor Celia, who had hoped to record some live guitar playing, was done in by the very institution for which she was so diligently toiling.

The first evening out from Alora was magical: we arrived at our destination, Ardales, by the light of the full moon. The electricity had failed and the *pueblo* stood out, an unearthly white against a drop curtain of black rock. Not a glimmer was to be seen and it appeared as a city of the dead. As we rode into the outskirts, all the lights went on again and the children, till then completely silent, started shrieking with delight.

* * *

Lest the tourist trade be adversely affected by what is to follow I must explain that there are excellent hotels in all the great sight-seeing centres and coastal resorts of modern Spain. The exchange being so much in our favour (autumn 1961), you can stay in a first-class hotel for the same *en pension* rates as in a third-class hotel in Italy.

The name *parador* which used to denote a large caravanserai for horses, mules, wagons and their drivers, is now given to special government-run hotels (though a few of the old type still survive) usually consisting of beautiful renaissance palaces or convents brought up to American standards of comfort.

On the other hand the rural inns of the *pueblos* have altered little since Ford's time and, according to him, since classical times. Thank God the end of all Spanish things has not yet come as the great man prophesied it would. The remoter corners of the peninsula are still 'not to be enjoyed by the over fastidious in the fleshly comforts'.*

There is still the *fonda*, a brand of hotel which is found in the larger *pueblos* and which caters for people only, not horses. The bedrooms contain from one to four beds apiece which are tolerably comfortable, though the mattresses and pillows often appear to be filled with walnuts (actually lumpy flock).† The eiderdown is unknown, so is the bedside mat. One pleasant respect in which these inns do differ from Ford's time lies in the complete absence of small bed-fellows. In six weeks touring I did not meet with a single bug or flea and not because '*Quien duerme bien no le pican pulgas*' (He who sleeps well is not bitten by fleas). Due to over-excitement and indigestion I often slept very badly.

The bedrooms of the *fonda* sometimes lead one into the other and at Almargen a strange gentleman occupied an inside one giving onto the corridor and having no windows, and I came next with one door leading into the gentleman's and the other into Mary's. The floors are of stone or rough cement and there is sometimes a spy-hole in one of them, or in the floor of the landing, about four inches in diameter, through which you get an excellent view of the room below and of its occupants.

The furniture consists of a couple of chairs, a tall chest-of-drawers, a distorting mirror, a few pegs fitting into some trellis work high up on the wall (one of which

* Ford: *op cit.*, ch. xv.
† *Ibid.*, ch. vi. Also Cervantes: *Don Quixote*, Book iii, ch. 2 (Everyman).

7

never fails to crash to the ground with whatever you hang on it) and an ingeniously designed washstand leaning well over to one side. This has an enamel basin resting in a crooked wooden frame, so that the water often spills onto the floor. Projecting from the frame on either side is some ornamental scroll work on which you may try in vain to perch your sponge and soap and toothbrush: within a matter of seconds they have fallen through the scroll work onto the floor.

The *posada* is an inn with stables attached, the animals being often better housed and better fed than the human beings. Both enter by the same front door, which in the smaller *posadas* leads directly into the living-room. Your horse is led through this into the great cavernous stables beyond, which are cool in summer and warm in winter. In the larger *posadas* there are big double doors, open during the day, which lead into a covered cobbled yard where the muleteers and the donkey boys sleep on straw palliasses. At the far end are the stables with rows of mangers, sometimes over a hundred, all along the walls with pegs above them (often the thigh bones of animals cemented in between the stones) to which you tie your halter rope. Borrow was fond of sleeping in mangers but if they were anything like the ones I saw, he must have curled up like a dog.*

On either side of the cobbled yard are the kitchen and dining-room and stairs leading up to the bedroom. The furnishing is similar to that of the *fonda* but in the more remote districts there is no chest-of-drawers, so that you have to keep your clothes in the saddle-bags, hung on the end of the bed, your books on the window-sill and risk hanging your coat and hat and camera on the wall-pegs which may or may not remain *in situ*. At least one of the bedrooms is used as a store for barley, maize, onions, almonds, pumpkins and pomegranates. There is seldom

* Borrow: *op. cit.*, Vol. I, chs. x and xi.

8

any glass in the windows. Ill-fitting and dilapidated wooden shutters keep out some of the draughts and all of the light, a feeble artificial variety of which is provided by a 15-watt bulb usually hung over the foot of your bed.

The *posada* often has the advantage over the *fonda* in that it possesses only stable sanitation. When the water variety is attempted it is always a dismal failure, partly because there is never any water laid on. You simply ladle it into the pan from a large stone jar, and the stink from the drains is overpowering. The Spaniards possess a great variety of talents but plumbing is not one of them.

The technique of using stable sanitation successfully and without undue strain on the nerves is as follows: when you want to enter the stable to attend to your horse, you open the door with a smile on your face, switch on the light and advance towards the animal, welcoming any help from your landlord or fellow-guest which may be offered. When, however, you wish to enter it for the other purpose you go towards the door with a look of grim determination upon your face, do not turn on the light, and slam the door hard behind you. Should you hear a giant pee-ing close by it is almost certain to be a mule or donkey: and when your eyes, growing used to the dim light, discern the figure of your landlady squatting in a corner, the custom is for both of you to roar with laughter as if this clandestine meeting were the most natural thing in the world, which indeed it is.

The menus in *fondas* and *posadas* differ little but whereas in the former meals are provided, in the latter the traveller can please himself: he can either bring his own food and cook it on the open kitchen fire, or he can eat what his landlady sets before him.

Breakfast consists of a species of doughnut ring (*churro*) fried in olive oil in the street or market-place and dipped in sugar. If the *pueblo* is too small for a *churro*-frier then you will get fried bread dipped in sugar or simply dry bread. In either case your food will be washed down with roasted barley 'coffee' which, apart from the fact that it is hot, has very little else to recommend it. What is called *café bueno*, which is real coffee, can be had in the local bar and nobody takes offence if you go and break your fast there, but in the small villages there isn't one.

The staple diet of rural Andalusia consists of vegetable soups and stews (*cocidos* and *pucheros*). These are made with a basis of dried chickpeas and different sorts of beans, all very high in protein, stewed together with potatoes, onions, pimientos, garlic and any available green vegetables. Sometimes the beans are replaced by rice, and now and then there will be the added thrill of lumps of fat pork. When eating these *cocidos* and *pucheros* day after day, week after week, the lack of relish is compensated for by the knowledge of how wholesome they are.

Fish soup is popular— fresh sardines or little mussels in their shells in a saffron-coloured broth with many cloves of garlic and bits of bread floating in it. Prawns, squids, hake, bream and fresh anchovies are also brought from the coast to the inland *pueblos* in Vespa vans two or three times a week.

The Spanish soup which is deservedly famous outside Spain, *gazpacho*, is always eaten cold during the summer months, fresh cucumber being one of its essential ingredients.

The home-cured hams of Spain are also famous throughout Europe and the exquisite flavour varies with the district, those of Estramadura taking the top place. Thick slices are eaten raw, not smoked, and are not easily dealt with by delicate digestions. One can however always ask for it fried, a practice which horrifies the connoisseur. Apart from the products of the pig, meat is rarely met with outside the tourist areas. Cattle are bred for ploughing or fighting and not for milking or eating. Karakul sheep are bred for the skins of the new-born lambs. Kid, hare, rabbit, chicken and partridge are occasional luxuries. I had rabbit twice in six weeks, chicken once and partridge three times.

Fresh eggs are everywhere plentiful and can be had boiled according to the number of minutes you dictate, or poached in oil, when they are served in a soup-plate floating in half an inch of it. This brings us to bread, the great mopper-up. Spanish bread is superlative and is a pleasure to eat dry, which is very fortunate as neither butter nor jam are to be had in the *pueblos* (though one can buy slabs of quince jelly which has the consistency of damson cheese and is a good stomach binder). It is all baked in flat, round crusty loaves in stone ovens preheated with brushwood, like the old brick ones of our farmhouses and bake-houses and cottages, some of which still survive. In colour it is just off-white, being not over-refined yet not over coarse and dark. It is eaten in prodigious quantities by the Spaniards and I took to it myself in a big way and after the first week forgot that there was such a thing as butter. To return to eggs, there is the famous *tortilla*, or Spanish omelette, which consists of fried potatoes and onions with beaten eggs poured onto them, fried on one side then tossed like a pancake and fried on the other. This can be leathery or light, according to the hand of the cook, and is actually at its best when eaten cold on a picnic. Many landladies can also do a tolerable version of a French omelette. Excellent salads and fresh fruit are available according to season.

Of Spanish wines, alas, I am not competent to write, having acquired a strong distaste for alcohol at the age of sixteen when I drank too much Vouvray on Shrove Tuesday at my school in Tours. Chapters XII and XIII of Ford's *Gatherings* still form, I am told, one of the best guides.

Posada cats are really useful animals for clearing up food which turns your stomach. Every *posada* has two or three of them (large proportion of tortoiseshells) to catch the rats and mice which would otherwise devastate the afore-mentioned bedroom stores. Many is the fish soup which I have cleared up with the aid of the *posada* cats, giving them most of the boiled sardines and sopping up the broth with bread and dropping it under the table. They do not appear to be fed regularly and are therefore invaluable collaborators with foreign travellers who are unaccustomed to many of the dishes set before them.

To sum up, *posada* life must be entered into in a spirit of adventure. The lack of modern comforts and gastronomic pleasures, which the average tourist demands, will soon be forgiven and forgotten if you decide to become a *posada* specialist: to enjoy, in each new inn you come to, the different distortions to which the mirror subjects your face; the angle at which the washstand leans over to left or right; the beauty of the pumpkins and pomegranates and pimientos drying in the spare bedroom; and the skill required to fill your hot-water with a soup ladle from a frying-pan—for the kettle is unknown in southern Spain.

On the preliminary tour all the arrangements were made and the bills paid under the expert guidance of Vicki Sumner and the only Spanish I spoke was to Pitirri, the gypsy groom. He taught me to sing the Hail Mary and also a lot of words pertaining to the feeding and shoeing of horses. Every morning before starting I would write out a vocabulary to be learnt while riding along. By the time I set off on my own tour, therefore, I was equipped with a good string of nouns such as barley, straw, girth, crupper, saddle, horse-shoe, blacksmith, but not more than six past participles: I have come, I have been, I have seen, I have suckled, I have read, I have eaten. I could never remember more than the present tenses of the two verbs 'to be' and the two verbs 'to have'.

On learning a language

Plunged into the heart of rural Andalusia I gauged my progress by the sermons I heard. The first one, delivered at Churriana in early October, was wholly incomprehensible; but by the end of November, after being on my own for a month, I could understand and enjoy the excellent preaching which is a great feature of Spanish church life—sermons of evangelical length lasting from thirty to forty minutes.

If you want to learn a language in middle age you must go back to the methods of childhood and pick it up largely by ear. To do this it is essential to live *alone* among the people who speak it: then come home and study your grammar books and have regular lessons. I tried to do this the other way round but owing to premature senile decay I could remember nothing from one lesson to the next. It was not until I lived and moved among Spaniards, far from any English people, that I started to speak and to understand their magnificent language, though Heaven knows I still have a lot to learn.

When Max Beerbohm* imperfectly understood a French literary lady at a dinner party in London, he simply said 'C'est vrai' when she had finished launching at him 'a particularly swift flight of winged words'. I found the magic Spanish word '*claro*' (clearly) far more reliable. For whereas Max Beerbohm was badly caught out, '*claro*' never once let me down, being a suitable comment on a positive, negative or interrogative sentence.

*　　　*　　　*

Having completed my entrancing conducted tour in the Serrania de Ronda I set about planning my solo ride. Thank God for Hercules Bellville who sent me to stay with his American friends Bill and Annie Davis in their

* Max Beerbohm: *And Even Now*, 'On Speaking French' (Heinemann).

13

villa near Malaga. They have a wonderful library of books on Spain and have together explored every corner of Andalusia accessible by car. Bill suggested that I make for Cazorla in the sierra of that name and Annie insisted that I visit Ubeda because of its architecture. I read up their *Guide Bleu* on that area and bought some very bad maps in Seville of the provinces of Granada and Jaén. My equipment I had hired from Antonio: an Andalusian saddle with triangular iron stirrups, beautiful leather *alforjas*, and a vast black oilskin Napoleonic-hooded coat. As to the horse, I had visions of a beautiful Arabian which of course I would call Sidi Habismilk after George Borrow's beloved stallion which he kept in the little silent square of Pila Seca in Seville. But I learned that pure-bred arabs in Spain to-day fetch Crabbet Park prices —£500 and upwards. Bill took me to see some nice-looking Hispano-Arabs at Torremolinos (belonging to a gypsy who hires them out) but they were very young, three and four years old, and I thought they would not stand up to a long tour carrying a lot of weight in rough country, and that they might well throw splints and go dead lame on me.

Then the Duke of Wellington very kindly wrote from England and said that I could borrow an animal off his farm near Illora. So, at the beginning of November, Bill and Annie motored me up to Molino del Rey, some eighteen miles north-west of Granada, with all my equipment, and there I met and stayed with the Duke's agent Eudo Tonsen-Rye and his wife Rosemary on the estate originally presented by the Spanish people to the Iron Duke for driving Napoleon out of Spain. There was a stableful of horses bedded on wheat straw and fed on home-grown oats and lovely lucerne hay. There were one or two part-bred arabs among them which might have deserved the noble name of Sidi Habismilk and my hopes ran high. But these were not for me. Eudo, an experienced horsemaster from Mallow, pointed out that they would soon lose condition on tour, standing in strange *posada* stables and being fed on barley and chopped straw. So he took me down to the home farm where there was a modern piggery, a fine herd of Friesians and a mule stud. Out of a barn a fifteen-hand bay mare was led, with one white sock and string-halt in the off hind. She was fat like a hunter at grass in midsummer and, but for her hogged mane, would have been a perfect Cuyp model. Not by any stretch of the imagination could she pass for Sidi Habismilk: she was the wrong sex and her face was convex instead of concave, denoting Spanish blood. Eudo explained that he had selected her for my tour because she was the greediest animal on the farm, a real good doer, and was accustomed to the fodder of the country— barley and barley straw chaff. She had only had one mule foal and had then proved barren and was used by the bailiff to hack around the estate. She was twelve years old, more or less equivalent in horse age to my fifty-one years. She was called La Marquesa, the Marchioness. So we were going exploring together—two middle-aged ladies in Andalusia.

*   *   *

GUY FAWKE'S DAY

It was Sunday and we all went to Mass in the little sham-Gothic estate chapel in the yard with the house servants and bailiffs and farm-hands and their families. Then we had a memorable breakfast of bacon and eggs and tea and toast and butter and marmalade, after which I went upstairs and by a heart-searching process of elimination finally decided on cramming the following things into my saddle-bags (my complete luggage for the coming month): Daily Missal, dictionary, Ford's *Gatherings*, Vol. I of *Don Quixote* in English, slim paper-

back of St Peter of Alcántara for Spanish reading practice, 1st and 2nd grades of the Spanish Catechism, two
large exercise books for diary and notes, writing-paper
and envelopes, sponge bag, hot-water bottle, 1 pair
pyjamas, 1 change of underclothes, 2 shirts, 1 mauve
jersey, 1 grey Terylene skirt rolled into an old stocking,
2 pairs stockings, 2 pairs socks, 4 hankies, and Mary
Clive's invaluable legacy—a plastic hang-up holdall divided into eight sections into which I put face cream,
powder, films, shoe-polish, mending things, Elastoplast,
tummy-trouble medicine, a comb, and some face tissues.

I wore lightweight jodhpurs, strong jodhpur boots
which I bought in Alora, a shirt and tie, and a grey
Sevillian hat to shade my eyes from the sun. At the last
minute Rosemary Tonsen-Rye lent me a small rucksack
into which I put an extra jersey, my picnic lunch and a
dandy brush (I carried this and my camera on my back).
In place of dees, Andalusian saddles have several pairs of
leather bootlaces dangling from them and with these I
tied my black oilskin cape and three-quarter-length tweed
coat onto the front of the saddle, together with my
bota (leather wineskin) containing lemonade, and hung
my *alforjas* over the high cantle behind.

At 11.30 a.m. I mounted the Marquesa and set off with
Eudo and one of the bailiffs in the direction of Illora.
After riding together for some three kilometres they left
me and I found myself alone with the fascinating problem of cross-country navigation in a land which was
completely strange to me. Suddenly I realised I had
learnt nothing of this (as intended) on my first tour
because Vicki and Pitirri knew the Serrania de Ronda so
well they never had to consult a map or ask the way. I
actually had two different maps of the provinces of
Granada and Jaén, scale 1 cm to 10 km on one, no scale
at all on the other. In comparing them I observed that
whereas one marked a certain village north of another,

the other would mark the same village south of it. Neither had any contours. One put in the names and heights of the chief sierras, the other didn't. One printed the main roads red and the secondary ones green, the other marked all the roads in black. Neither recorded mule-tracks, which were the only roads along which I wanted to ride. How then did I proceed? In the morning before starting I would decide on the village where I meant to spend the night. I would write this down in block capitals in a small pocket note-book together with the names of the one or two other villages I had to pass through to reach it. I used block capitals to avoid having to put on spectacles and I referred to these names continually because owing to my failing memory I could never remember them for two minutes together. I would get good directions from my starting-point in the morning and after that took Annie Davis' excellent advice: 'You are never alone for long in Spain,' she had said, 'you will always find a ploughman or a shepherd who will tell you the way.' In point of fact these people know the tracks from their own village to the next but have seldom heard of the one beyond it: neither will they tell you how many kilometres it is to a certain place, but how many hours of riding, five kilometres to the hour being their measure. I found this dead accurate at a walking pace but if we trotted and cantered a bit we could do eight kilometres to the hour except over steep sierras when we were rather slower than donkeys. When you want to ascertain the distance from one place to another therefore you ask '¿Cuanta hora de camino?' (How many hours of riding?). The sun is another great comfort in cross-country navigation. I was riding due east on my outward journey to Cazorla and as long as the sun worked round my right shoulder all day and set in my back I knew I was getting always closer to my destination. What makes riding in this part of Spain so marvellous is the complete absence of barbed wire. You can take your direction from the sun and ride straight to a place with no man-made obstacles to hinder you. There are of course natural obstacles such as rivers and ravines but they are nothing like so unpleasant as barbed wire, the scourge of the English countryside.

After leaving Eudo I followed his directions to Illora, skirted round the south of the Moorish fort and rode along an unmetalled country lane through olive groves for five or six kilometres. I had three villages on my block-capital list but had an open mind as to where I should spend the first night. From the map, Moclín appeared to be in a direct line to the other two. Actually it turned out to be well to the north of the line and I should not have gone near it. But it was so beautiful that I am very glad that I did. The splendid inaccuracy of the maps led me to many such places which I would otherwise have missed.

Across the main Cordoba–Granada road there was a broad earth track, suitable for carts as well as pack animals, leading over rich plough-land, part of the fertile *vega* of Granada. I was looking forward to a canter along it, but on asking a ploughman the way to Moclín he pointed to a low range of rocky hills to the north, up which I could vaguely discern a path ascending steeply. So I turned the Marquesa's head and up we went. Near to the top of this, our first pass, I dismounted and ate my cold *tortilla* while the mare cropped the mountain herbs and my two apple cores. Then I led her on along the now indistinct goat path which sometimes appeared but more often disappeared among the rocks on the steep side of the hill. I mounted, hoping to see the path better from above, but it became narrow and the ground sloped away so steeply to our left that I thought the Marquesa's feet must surely shoot from under her. I dismounted uphill, on the off side, started a landslide and slid right under her belly! She was very surprised, moved forward and in-advertently trod on my left calf. I finally managed to scramble to my feet again and somehow we slithered down to the plough level together, when I returned to the saddle, and after riding over ridges and furrows for some two kilometres we came to a country road which led past a Moorish watch-tower, a cemetery, and a large *Guardia Civil* barracks to Moclín. On the outskirts of the *pueblo* there was a stone drinking trough but the Marquesa would not drink. Above us there was a large Moorish fort and across the *vega* to the south was the great range of the Sierra Nevada, the peaks powdered with the first falls of snow. I had only ridden twelve kilometres but decided to stay here the night. I rode up to where four old men were gossiping and asked, 'Is there a *posada* here?' No, there was no *posada*. 'Is it then possible to stay anywhere?' One of them thought for a moment and then said that it was. He led me down a little cobbled street and spoke to a young woman outside a house, who turned out to be his daughter-in-law Euge-nia. She angelically agreed to put up the Marquesa and myself for the night.

We had some difficulty in persuading the old girl to go in through the front door which was rather low and she was rather tall. I pulled and coaxed while the old man pushed and shouted. Together we got her safely into the living-room of the little house: the floor was paved with stone but a path of cobbles led across it from the front door to the stable door at the back through which we led her to her quarters for the night. Mean-while Eugenia's husband Fernando had appeared, a gentle young man of twenty-seven with a saintly smile. He set about getting water for the Marquesa, chaff from the loft and barley from the village shop. I asked him to buy her four kilos which cost twenty *pesetas*, the price varying from place to place between five and six *pesetas* a kilo. Another door led out of the stable into a hen and pig yard, rising in three wide cobbled terraces to a rough stone wall at the top. There was no loo. You could take your choice of the stable or the yard.

Somewhere around 4 p.m. Eugenia and Fernando sat down to their lunch of *cocido* which they ate out of a bowl in the middle of the table, each having a spoon but no plate. I was of course asked to share it but told them I had eaten a good lunch on my little sierra.

In the big open fireplace of her living-room Eugenia lit a fire of olive twigs and banked up barley straw chaff. I thought of all the wood feeding the flames which were consuming the thousands of guys up and down England that night on giant bonfires—wood which would be worth its weight in gold in Spain. But Eugenia knew nothing of our great anti-popery festival so she did not grudge our children their bonfires. She boiled some cereal and goat's milk together for Maria, her eight months' old baby, who ate it with relish and was then put to the breast while her mother and I had a nice talk on the merits of breast-feeding. I was told that lots of girls in the village who were quite well off and had plenty to eat protested that they had not enough milk to feed their babies. This seems odd as there are no distractions such as theatres and dances to tempt them away from home. Interesting point: has T.V. led to an increase of nursing mothers in England?

We had our supper at about 9.30 p.m. consisting of very good broth followed by a French omelette which Eugenia insisted on making especially for me. Having been in service for five years in Malaga before she married she had learnt a lot of cooking. We also had fresh sardines dipped in flour and fried in olive oil. After supper an old lady came in, wrapped in a black shawl, and we all knelt round the table and joined in a novena to St Rita, the patron Saint of housewives, Fernando reading out the prayers from a little book. Eugenia told me afterwards that her intention was for the recovery of her husband from his deafness. I was given the best bedroom next to the living-room, Eugenia making up her double bed with clean embroidered sheets for me. Maria's cot was moved next door and her mother and father slept on the floor in front of the fire while the grandfather slept in the bedroom on the first floor.

Monday, November 6

Fernando went off to work at 8 a.m., having break-fasted off a poached egg floating in broth. He wound a piece of white calico round each foot before putting on leather sandals, pairs of which I subsequently saw hanging in every village shop. He was a day labourer: yester-day no man had hired him but to-day somebody had.

After my breakfast of delicious crusty bread and barley coffee I asked Eugenia to boil me an egg for my lunch and I went to one of the three village shops to buy some lemons and Marie biscuits. At 11 a.m. I set off, the old grandfather helping me to saddle up. He then walked beside me till we reached the outskirts of Moclín, and put me on the right track which zig-zagged steeply down between two craggy hills. I got off and led the Marquesa. We passed several patches of pale mauve autumn crocus whose stamens, when dried, are called saffron. Curiously enough I did not observe any cultivated strips of this Spanish crocus though I saw plenty some years ago in the Abruzzi. No wonder saffron is so expensive when you think how many flowers are needed to sacrifice their stamens to make up a single ounce of this culinary spice.

We passed through the small straggling village Los Olivares, which was not marked on either of my maps. I enquired about the mule-track to Colomera and was

directed onto one bordered by flowering aloes and cling-
ing to the base of the little sierras we had ascended
yesterday further back. Got a crick in the neck from
repeatedly turning round to look at Moclín, a Castle in
Spain perched on the edge of what appeared to be a
sheer precipice. I had slept up there in a fairy-tale and
could not imagine how the mare and I had descended such
a cliff wall. We had lunch on a hillock a hundred yards off
the mule-track in an Elysian landscape dominated by the
great Sierra Nevada across the fertile plain of Granada.
The Marquesa cropped grass and acorns for which she
apparently had a passion: there were clumps of holly
oaks on our little hill.

During our lunch breaks I always removed the snaffle
bridle, leaving the noseband on for moral effect. I also
removed the saddle-bags but not the saddle as it was too
heavy for me to lift on again. I brought no corn with me
as I believe she enjoyed a change of diet and although
an English horse might have snorted in derision at
Spanish grazing, she seemed to do herself very well on it.
I never let go an opportunity to let her water at irrigation
canals, streams or village drinking-troughs. As to drink
for myself, I found that I was without it, for the string
of my *bota* must have slipped over the saddle-bow and
disentangled itself from the bootlaces. Perhaps it was
covered with shame at being asked to carry lemonade
instead of wine and had deliberately jumped off and
hidden itself among the aloes or blackberry bushes of
the wayside. So I sat and sucked a lemon under a little
holly oak and ate my hard-boiled egg with bread and
Marie biscuits and some of the delicious milky almonds
which Eugenia had given me as a parting present. These
I cracked between two stones. One is never without
stones on which to crack nuts in Spain.

By 2 p.m. we were in Colomera, unimpressive from
this western side, but from the north-east along our road

to Benalua, wonderfully dramatic—a large church just below a Moorish fortress with the village houses clustering round the foot of the hill. I was walking along leading the Marquesa as I always did for two or three miles every day to stretch my legs and take some of the weight off her back, when I caught up with three men, one of whom asked me home for the night, saying he had a wife and five grown-up children but that there would be room for me too. He got on behind a boy on a large donkey and we turned off the road and crossed the river running through the valley and jogged along a lovely cart-track bordered by poplars and with the houses of smallholders at fairly regular intervals all along it.

After riding for two miles we came to Francisco Martinez' house which was called Santo Domingo and consisted of a long bungalow built by himself and his family, the back rooms being carved out of the hill behind it. At one end there was a stable for two mules, at the other a pig-sty. The Marquesa was put into the stable and fed with barley and chaff but when the two mules came home from the fields she had to move over into the sty. It was actually the same size and shape as the stable but was inhabited by two pigs to which, like all her race, the Marquesa strongly objected. I don't know how many well-directed kicks the poor pigs received in the night.

The large square Señora insisted on my having a second lunch with her husband at 5 p.m. He ate raw home-cured ham but I asked for it to be fried: we also had fried eggs, plenty of bread, and little white grapes. Then my host went out shooting and I accompanied him across the river through groves of young poplars but we saw nothing but goats. He seemed very contented with his lot. His sons did all the work of the smallholding and his wife and three daughters all the work of the house while he himself led the life of a gentleman of leisure, living on the produce of his land, walking into his local *pueblo* every day for a gossip and a drink, and going out shooting whenever he felt so inclined.

My next social engagement was coffee and a gossip in the house of some neighbours a little further along the track. We all sat round the big open fireplace in which burned the usual fuel of straw chaff and olive prunings. When it got dark the beautiful wife of my host lit a little open iron lamp containing home-produced olive oil. It was of the same design as those carried by the wise and foolish virgins in Byzantine mosaics, and gave very little light and smoked a lot, but there was no electricity in this valley and burning your own oil was cheaper than buying candles. While I drank my barley coffee the man and his wife and two of their friends drank wine from a *porrón*, the communal glass wine-jar with a long spout which is passed from person to person but never touches the lips: the wine is poured into the mouth from at least six inches away. I had my first try at doing this and the wine went all over my face.

My host was a very good-looking man but difficult to understand; by insisting on his speaking very slowly, however, and repeating many phrases, I gathered that there used to be bandits in the surrounding hills who would come in and demand half the food and money in the house. They were a great nuisance and were mostly men from the losing side in the war, but they were finally cleared out in 1955. I told him that my husband had been very worried about the bandit question as many English people were under the impression that they were still rampant in Andalusia. He had written to implore me to take out an insurance policy with a bank in Seville as he would not have enough money to pay my ransom. But he was reassured when I asked Eudo Tonsen-Rye to write and tell him that there was no danger any more and that the people through whose country I was going to travel were peaceful and law-abiding.

Early morning liqueur

I walked home to supper at 9 p.m. and we had a very good *puchero*—vegetable stew. We each had a spoon and ate out of a bowl in the middle of the round table and drank out of the communal wine-jar. I also had a glass of delicious spring water. Places here are known by their water and you speak of such and such a place having a *buena agua* as if it were wine. Lobo, the family dog, a large friendly mongrel, was given a big bowl of stew for his supper with bits of bread broken into it. I was again given the best bedroom, lit by a wise and foolish virgin lamp, and divided from the living-room by a curtain instead of a door.

TUESDAY, NOVEMBER 7

At 8.30 a.m. a hand was thrust through the curtain holding a little glass of aniseed liqueur. I thanked my host very much, drank a sip or two and poured the rest into my washing water.

We had a wonderful breakfast of fried ham and eggs and bread and barley coffee and I was given a second glass of liqueur which I managed to pour unseen into a handy pot of geraniums when my host went out to help harness the mules. The two little pigs, released from their sty and the company of their disdainful guest, kept running in and out of the room.

It was a fresh sunny morning and I wore my red sweater when I set off soon after 10 a.m. along a little path which led backwards and forwards across the river and up onto the unmetalled road to Benalua. As I was trotting past a mule cart the driver shouted that I was losing something. It turned out to be the dandy brush, so I thanked him warmly and got off and put it back in my rucksack which had come untied at the top.

I had three names on my block-capital list for to-day: Benalua, Dehesas Viejas and Torre Cardela. It was at

Benalua that St John of the Cross, on one of his mule-tours as Vicar-Provincial of Andalusia, threw down a hat between two men who were fighting to the death with knives and stopped them and made them kiss one another's feet as a sign of forgiveness.* I rode through this pretty little *pueblo* and out onto the far side where there was an enormous chaff rick, at least fifty feet long. I cannot understand how the chaff sticks together. Building a hay rick is difficult enough but I wouldn't know how to begin on a chaff rick.

Passing a group of labourers, both men and women, lifting sugar beet and loading it into an enormous lorry drawn up by the side of the field, I asked them the way to Dehesas Viejas, and was told there was a good mule-track a couple of kilometres up the main road to the left. I stopped and had a fizzy lemonade at a wayside bar—Citrania—quite the best mineral I have ever drunk, ginger beer not excepted. The main road was tarred, but they have a civilised rule in Spain that the verge of all such roads must be left unmetalled on either side for the benefit of beasts of burden.

The mule-track was easy to find and led across beautiful hilly farmland. I saw the sower going forth to sow: there were plenty of rocks for his seed to fall on, also my path with briers alongside it. On the good soil the seed was not harrowed in as in England, but ploughed in by six teams of mules, a pair to each plough. We had our lunch break in a grassy glade with plenty of little oak trees and acorns. I followed the mare's example and ate some of these but they were bitter and not a patch on Eugenia's almonds.

After lunch, as we were continuing along the track, I saw a ploughman and his team working at such an angle on the side of a steep hill that I realised with awe that Spaniards are not subject to the law of gravity. Neither are

* Crisogono de Jesus: *Life of St John of the Cross*, pp. 235-6 (Longman).

their mules. The mule-track was clearly defined to De-hesas Viejas, a sad, deserted-looking village through which I rode northwards, and then turned off the road onto a track leading towards the east which satisfied my sense of direction and put the sun where it ought to be. I had asked a group of men on the outskirts of the *pueblo* for directions to Torre Cardela but they never seemed to have heard of it.

We followed the track of my choice through hilly olive groves; then the hills rolled out into broad down-like sweeps and there were no more olive trees planted on them, no landmarks of any sort: everywhere you looked the landscape was uniform—a desert of plough without a blade of grass to be seen. The track reached the top of a hill from where I could see a great black wall of mountain to the south, the Sierra Arana, accord-ing to my map, with snow-capped peaks of the Sierra Nevada rising behind it. The sun was correctly behind my right shoulder when the track became a 'T' turning sharply north and south. To the east where I wanted to go there was a steep hill of plough. Very annoyed I turned to the left and sank back into a valley where without any warning a little lost *pueblo* appeared where none had been before, complete with church and the faint cries of playing children. This was Domingo Perez which I had intended to bypass. I wondered whether I had suddenly become psychic and was having a vision of a village which did not really exist, but I was brought to earth by the very material sight of two Civil Guards, one enormously fat, with rifles slung over their shoulders. I thought they would wonder who on earth I was and would demand to see my papers so I started to recite the little piece Eudo had taught me: 'I am English, I am on a riding tour in this province. I have come from the farm of the English Duke of Wellington and Ciudad Rodrigo, this is his mare . . .'! '*Muy bien muy bien!*' said the circular

Guard and did not ask for my papers. He pointed out the mule-track to the right at the bottom of the hill which he told me was the way to Torre Cardela. We rode happily along for the next five kilometres, forded a river where the Marquesa had a nice drink and on the far side my track turned bang south. I took my bearings and knew that I should go straight ahead where there was a hill at right angles to the ground, and not be drawn to the Sierra Arana though all roads seemed to lead to it. So I again rode northwards along an indistinct track which soon deteriorated into a goat path leading along the edge of a dried-up stream which wound in and out of a deep gully between steep hills, the tops of which were ploughed. But it was evening and the ploughmen had all gone home with their mules and their dogs and there was not even a bird to be seen or heard. The sun kept dodging about all round us as we wound our worried way through the silent deserted gully, for we were completely lost. Sometimes the thorn bushes were so thick across the path that I had to get off and tread them down before the Marquesa would proceed. On one of these occasions I remounted from the off-side putting my left foot, out of habit, into the stirrup and landed back to front in the saddle. The gully seemed interminable and to pretend that the path was a path any more was simply wishful thinking: it was alarmingly obvious that it had petered out altogether. It was getting towards sundown and I began to think we would have to spend the night in this valley of the dead. There was no water and just a very few dusty weeds for the Marquesa's supper, a lemon and a good supply of Eugenia's almonds for mine. I got extremely annoyed with St Christopher for getting us into such a pickle. Then I knelt down, squashed between thorn bushes, and prayed to the Blessed Virgin to help us, pointing out that it was evidently too big a task for St Christopher whose rightful province it was to look after travellers. I looked up and noticed that the almost perpendicular hill above us was ploughed half-way down. I started to scramble up it on all fours, pulling the mare behind me. By superhuman efforts we reached the plough level and then plodded our weary way up to the top of the hill. About a kilometre to the south-east stood a large white farmhouse. No ship-wrecked sailor was ever more thankful to see a sail.

It took us about twenty minutes of panting up and down to reach it, and to my delight I found it stood beside the secondary road I had hoped to cross two hours earlier. A woman standing by the door told me that it was an hour's ride to Torre Cardela and that a good track led off the road to the right a little further up, so we rode north for a kilometre or so and then turned due east onto the mule-track which was broad and clearly defined and evidently meant to get somewhere important. It wound round the low hills past several large farmhouses and I saw a small boy galloping bareback on a donkey driving in some hobbled horses from pasture. The sun beat us to it and set with the most glorious after-glow I ever remember seeing since leaving Delhi. It was between moons and the darkness came down rather suddenly but the *camino de mulo* had banked-up edges so was easy to follow and I saw the headlights of a car in the valley so that I knew we were approaching the main road and the *pueblo* we were making for. The track descended gently and in twenty minutes or so some white houses became dimly discernible on either side of us. I asked the way to the *posada* and was directed across the untarred main road. The large double doors were open and led into a covered cobbled yard at the far end of which was a long manger against the rough stone wall with a few mules and donkeys tied to pegs above it. The landlord unsaddled the Marquesa and led her to water and when she returned she fairly tucked into her *cebada y paja.* There was plenty of deep litter for her to roll and rest on.

All the children of the *pueblo* seemed to have collected in the covered yard and I took refuge in the living quarters to the left: a very high room, one end of which was used for dining and the other for cooking, there being the usual great open fireplace with a twig and straw fire. I was then taken up to a double room on the first floor with a light unusually near the bed, one chair, a few wall-pegs and an absolutely up-to-standard *posada* wash-stand leaning well over to the left.

Supper was at the 'cosy-table', which is always round with a wooden platform underneath it six inches off the ground, in the middle of which a brazier fits into a hole specially made to receive it. Into this brazier hot cinders are scooped from the open fire and your toes toast deliciously while a thick baize tablecloth covers your knees. The other guests were a simple young hawker who travelled the countryside selling his goods off a donkey, and a tough young troglodyte from Guadix who had left his family at home in a cave while he buzzed around on his 'moto' selling socks and shirts. He was the wit of the party and made a lot of jokes which I laughed at when everybody else did. We had saffron yellow fish broth with a lot of fresh sardines and bits of bread and cloves of garlic in it, followed by the usual eggs poached in half an inch of olive oil; they were actually a cross between a poached and a fried egg. I liked to mop up the yolk mixed with the oil on bits of bread, according to the custom of the country. Afterwards we all sat round the hearth and one of the daughters of the house knitted a sock on two needles which she said she would afterwards sew together. Another one did some writing practice. I told everybody as much as my Spanish would allow of my family history and then, having satisfied the demands of good manners, I wrote my diary. I always fed the

Marquesa last thing before going to bed in keeping with
the best Cervantean tradition (as when the carrier went
down in the middle of the night to give his mules their
second course):* thus she got three regular feeds daily,
the first at 8 a.m., the second as soon as we got in in the
evening which was any time between 5 and 7 p.m. and
the third between eleven and twelve at night. I had put
up her barley to two kilos a feed so that she was getting
six a day, that is a good thirteen pounds English measure.
I always had a fight with my host over the manger to
stop him putting in too much chopped straw, as I had
worked out a very practical system whereby I put the
mare's corn into one manger together with three or four
double handfuls of chaff, everything well mixed together.
Then I filled up the neighbouring manger with chaff and
tied her to a peg from which she could get her nose into
either manger at will. In this way she would eat up all her
corn and then help herself to roughage as she pleased.
The custom of the country is to sprinkle a little corn into
a lot of chaff but I wanted to be certain that the mare got
her full corn ration before stuffing herself up with *paja*.
Her mid-day feed usually consisted of grazing only:
grass and acorns when they were to be found, and herbs
in the mountains, especially a little one which looked
prickly but wasn't, locally called *celvero*.

WEDNESDAY, NOVEMBER 8

Went to Mass at 9.30 a.m. having ascertained the time
on the previous evening. There was one of the most
realistic figures of Our Lord carrying His Cross in this
church that I have yet seen: life-size, dressed in a long
purple robe edged with gold and having a shoulder-
length wig of real brown hair—these *pasos* are carried
through the streets in the Holy Week processions. At

* Cervantes: *op. cit.*, Book III, ch. 2 (Everyman).

9.40 a little altar-boy came up very politely and said that the Mass would start a bit late as the *cura* was just getting up. At 9.55 the *cura* appeared with his little red and white Tintoretto dog which heard Mass from the sacristy, after which it walked up and down the aisle impatient for its master to unvest, but never entered the sanctuary. When the *cura* reappeared I went up and asked him if there was anywhere in the *pueblo* where I could buy a rosary as I had left mine under my pillow at Santo Domingo. He said there wasn't and pulled one out of his pocket and asked me to accept it. I was deeply touched and very grateful as I hate being without one on a journey.

After a lovely breakfast of fried bread dipped in sugar and a huge cup of real coffee, my nice fat landlady made me a Spanish omelette for a picnic lunch which we wrapped in some brown paper with two pieces of fried bread over from breakfast and two bananas: what a *fête champêtre!*

We set off later than I intended and the whole village, including the *cura*, came to see me off. I had the humiliating experience of having to ask for a chair to facilitate mounting. Nobody laughed. I made a royal exit from the *pueblo* raising my right hand in salutation to the crowd with the sound of the beautiful Andalusian farewell ringing in my ears: '*Vaya Usted con Dio-o-o-o*' (May you go with God).

In a cowardly way I decided to keep to the unmetalled country road, thirty kilometres of it, through a desert region with a vast and terrifying canyon some way away to my right, as I did not want to repeat my experience of getting lost in it. When I say desert, I mean that it looked very little different from the Syrian one but was actually arid ploughland, not sand. There were very few olive trees to start with, then none at all, and I was disgusted to see several large tractors, one pulling disc harrows with a chain harrow tied on behind. We met the Spanish railways delivery donkey with packing cases tied onto its back and led by a little man in a grey uniform and peaked hat, and passed two farm lorries and two young men in a little Seat car who waved to me. A little further on I rode over a level-crossing which turned out to be the only railway to cross my path in a month of riding. We trotted a good bit and while walking I was able to do my homework on *Don Quixote* as the scenery was monotonous.

I rode through the lovely *pueblo* of Pedro Martinez and watered the Marquesa at the *fuente* in a little central plaza out of which a cobbled street ascended almost at right angles.

I must now digress a bit about *pueblos*. The word *pueblo* (people) is the name given to a country village or town consisting of a few hundred inhabitants or a few thousand, and up to thirty thousand.* Some of the larger ones, for example Ubeda (22,000 inhabitants), contain churches and palaces of great distinction and are tourist-ridden as a result. But in the smaller ones (population of 2,000 to 3,000), their charm consists, not in any outstanding architectural features, but in the way they have grown up over the centuries into a beautiful homogeneous pattern, all the work of craftsmen, nothing mass-produced.

The houses vary from one to three storeys in height and are built of local stone, and although the walls are plastered and whitewashed the individual shapes of the stones often stand out and form patterns of literally infinite variety. The roofing is all of unglazed yellowish-pink tiles. The better houses round the plaza and the neighbouring streets have iron balconies on the first floor with pots of flowers standing on them. Outside some of the smaller houses there are often little open courtyards

* *cf.* J. A. Pitt-Rivers: *The People of the Sierra*, ch. 1, p. 7 (Weidenfeld and Nicholson).

surrounded by low white walls, in which women sit and sew and children play. Sometimes they are shaded by a vine trained over a trellis.

The beauty of the little *pueblo* is the beauty of texture. In their own individual way, our English villages had just this quality before 'Progress' marched into them with ill-designed council houses and hideous bungalows all fitted with identical steel window-frames and mass-produced tiles.

Pedro Martinez is a typical but not outstanding *pueblo*, yet as I rode up and down its cobbled streets, passing traffic on four legs instead of on four wheels, and saw a handsome lean old lady seated in her forecourt, dressed in black and bending over her sewing, I was so transported by the harmony of the whole pattern—people, houses, donkeys, mules, tassels, tiles and cobbles—that I wished those minutes had been years.

To the north of the little town is an enormous cobbled parade ground (perhaps an outsize threshing-floor?) on which I saw twenty long low ricks of green stuff tied in bunches. Some men with a snow-white donkey mare, her little jennet foal at foot, were in the process of building the last rick. They told me it was *esparto grass*! At last I had seen the stuff that is described in every travel book on Spain.

A conference was held and it was decided that I should keep to the road, as the mule-track only saved about four kilometres and was said to be very difficult to follow. When I saw the nature of the country I had to traverse towards evening, I was grateful for this advice. We proceeded across a more interesting desert than the morning one, and met some donkeys laden with esparto grass, and then a string of mules and packhorses laden with fir branches for the baker's ovens. Having learned from Pitirri the words of command given to animals I leapt from the Marquesa and said 'Brrrrrrrrr' as loudly as I could, whereupon the whole string stopped dead as if frozen to the ground; the men were surprised but delighted to pose for a photograph. This was the technique I always adopted when I wanted to get a good transparency for Women's Institute lectures.

There was no lovely glade for our lunch break, but eventually we found a bank covered with *celvero* which the mare grazed while I ate my *tortilla* and bananas. I could not face the fried bread, neither could the Marquesa, so I wrapped it up again in greasy brown paper and kept it for our next *posada* cats.

As we rode on into some hills, sparsely planted with stone-pines from which the mules had received their loads, the same car passed us which I had seen in the morning and once more the occupants waved delightedly. About three kilometres further on a boy bicycled up to us from a white farmhouse standing back from the road and said his master would be very pleased if I went in, so I rode up to find my friends of the little Seat car. The younger of the two, aged about twenty-five, was the owner of the farm and offered me wine and liqueurs. I knew it was useless asking for my favourite drink (for which at that moment I would have given my *alforjas*) in this ginger-beerless land, so I asked instead for lemonade but had to be content with 'coke'. He then asked all about my journey and I did my piece. He seemed very surprised I was riding alone. I said: 'Many Englishwomen are mad.' He said: 'No, very brave.' My bosom swelled with pride but I tried to explain how I thanked God for a plain middle age and how it was not brave for a female of fifty-one to ride through a beautiful friendly country where she was welcome wherever she went.

My host, who, having a car, measured distances in kilometres instead of in riding-hours, told me I had still ten to go to reach Villanueva de las Torres where I wanted to spend the night, and that it would take me a long time as the road descended very steeply for the last five. The sun would win the race again.

We rode on through the severe Piero della Francesca landscape of beautifully modelled white hills with black pines dotted frugally over them. I noticed that the ominous black canyon which had kept its distance to the right all day was now swinging round to the front. We rounded a bend and the whole of hell was spread out before us in the most extraordinary Doré picture you could fear to see—mile upon mile of completely bare hills set in a maze of shadowy gullies and gorges. It was the lunar landscape of southern Tuscany on a stupendous scale; a desert to intoxicate St Jerome and his lion; to drive the romantic painters of all ages to a frenzy. The sun began to set and the infernal regions glowed red and purple and orange, and I had to descend into them.

The stony road wound down and down in a series of hairpin bends and soon we were enveloped in the blanket of the moonless night. I got off and led the Marquesa because I thought she might inadvertently step over a precipice. It seemed to be tempting providence to break such silence by our footsteps: something unpleasant must be lurking in the inky depths of those ravines, waiting to pounce on us. Then, without any warning at all, there appeared a hundred holes with lights in them in the middle of the shadowy hills, and the screams of demons filled the night.

I had come upon a colony of troglodytes.

*　　*　　*

I sat in the *posada* in hell holding court with eight young men while my landlady went upstairs to prepare my room. When you are still in the elementary stages of learning a language your only hope is to talk yourself, to prevent people talking to you, as they are sure to introduce tenses with which you are not yet familiar. So I added to my usual set piece by giving as long an account of myself and my family and my travels in Spain as I could. How I wished I had mastered the imperfect! I was completely confined to the present tense, to one present and six past participles. . . .

'I am English, I am on a tour in these mountains, I have come from the farm of the English Duke of Wellington and Ciudad Rodrigo. That (pointing to the stable) is his mare. I have come from London to Madrid in an aeroplane. I have seen the museum of the Prado and also Toledo. *Muy bonito Toledo.* From Madrid I have been in an aeroplane to Malaga. I have been in the house of two American friends in Churriana, a *pueblo* near Malaga. I have been by bus to Granada where I have seen the Alhambra and the Generalife and the Cathedral and Cartuja. *Muy bonita Granada.* I have been in a train to Cordoba and have seen the Mesquita. Then I have been on a twelve-day riding-tour in the Serrania de Ronda staying at Ardales, Ariarte, Almargen, Ronda, Cueve de la Pileta, Zahara de los Membrillos and le Burgos. I have been with five other English ladies. Then I have been in an aeroplane to Seville. I have seen the Cathedral and many other churches and the House of Pilate with very beautiful tiles. *Muy bonito Sevilla.* Then I have been to the farm of the English Duke of Wellington and Ciudad Rodrigo near Illora from whence comes my mare. Sunday I have been to Moclín, Monday to Colomera, Wednesday to Torre Cardela . . .' No sign of my landlady. 'My husband is in Australia, he is a poet. I have a daughter of nineteen, she is a *mecanografa* in London. She stays with the first cousin of my husband. I have a son of twenty-four, he is a musician in London . . .' Still no sign of my landlady. 'In Spain you fight bulls (*toros*), in England we hunt foxes (*zorros*). We hunt the foxes with a lot of dogs . . .'

'Do you hunt them for their skins?'

'No, the dogs eat the skins.'

Silence. Surely I had been talking for twenty minutes? And still no sign of my landlady. But this monologue gave the lie to my audience: all eight young men started to talk to me at once, thinking that I could understand their language as well as I appeared to speak it. *'Claro'* I said at intervals: *'claro'*, though Heaven knows their meaning was far from clear. At last my landlady came down the stone stairs and announced that my room was ready. I followed her back up again and she led me into a little single bedroom with a rough stone floor, no glass in the windows, no chest-of-drawers, not even a distorting or any other kind of mirror, and an enamel basin in a simple iron frame in place of the usual wooden *posada* washstand. I hung my *alforjas* over the end of the bed and my coat and hat and plastic holdall onto the pegs fixed on a trellis to the wall. To my surprise none came crashing to the ground. I laid my books and diaries and writing materials in a row on the nice wide window-sill and felt very content with my lot.

After eating a large *tortilla* and a slice of melon for supper I went and called on the *párroco* to ask the time of Mass. He said it would be at 9 a.m. I did not go to his house but to the cave-dwelling of a middle-aged widow opposite the *posada*, where he had all his meals. It was approached through a double iron gate up a garden path bordered with flower-beds and had a built-up façade of whitewashed stone. The living-room was one of the most friendly and comfortable I had yet seen in Spain, with cushioned rocking-chairs on either side of the open fireplace and a cosy-table in the middle. The *párroco* was a tall, good-looking young man but very shy.

I went to bed at 11.30 p.m. with a bottle of white wine as a sleeping draught, as I had been sleeping very badly due to over-excitement. Swallowed five or six mouthfuls, read a little, then felt drowsy. Just as I was dropping happily off after midnight there was a clatter in the stone passage followed by a loud knock on the door. I sat up with a start and shouted 'Adelante!' as I switched on the light. In marched two Civil Guards with carbines slung over their shoulders, followed by my landlord who was embarrassed and apologetic. I was thrilled. At last I should be able to produce the Marquesa's papers: for all Spanish horses and mules have identity papers with the names of their breeders and any change of ownership recorded on them to facilitate the police in case of theft. I dug out the plastic sponge-bag hidden in the depths of my *alforjas*, extracted my passport from it and the mare's papers, and handed them to the moustached leader of the two Guards. He looked far longer and asked far more questions about her papers than about mine, which I endeavoured to answer as best I could. Then he wanted to know what I was doing here, so I started off on my piece: 'I am English, I am on a tour in these Sierras; I have come from . . .' During my recitation both the Guards lit cigarettes. Then the leader started to examine my few books on the window-sill. 'Ah! I see you must be a Catholic as you have this Missal? *Muy bien, muy bien.*' And they all left the room.

Thursday, November 9

In this village I at last discovered the Mass mystery in Spain: the church bell is rung three times. First of all about three-quarters of an hour before the Holy Sacrifice is due to start, then a second time about twenty minutes later, then the third and final time when the priest goes into the sacristy to vest. If he has overslept, nobody minds because they go by the bells, but it is very easy to lose count and often people say to you, 'Was that the second bell or the third?' I went along to church at 9 a.m. and

Mass started at 9.15 just after the third bell. Half a dozen girls aged about twelve or thirteen sat in the front pew and one of them handed out dialogue Mass cards called in Spanish *Misa participada*. The phonetic spelling, to try to get people to pronounce the Latin correctly, was most extraordinary. In addition to the girls, five or six women were present. Only the girls and I and the little boy serving the Mass did the responses. Obviously the older women could not read.

The village church at Don Diego has been rebuilt since the civil war in a pleasant unadorned classical style with a nave separated from the aisles by two rows of round arches. The whole building is whitewashed both inside and out and the east end is a windowless wall with a life-size crucifix hanging above the altar. This to my mind is the ideal retablo. At Mass I do not want to be distracted by vivid carvings of poor St John being boiled in oil nor of the catholic kings conquering Granada. God knows I have enough distractions as it is of one kind and another. A large crucifix helps me more than anything else to concentrate on the matter in hand, the sacrifice of Calvary.

This being a poor little church, it is not cluttered up with images. Nevertheless there are two niches on opposite sides of the nave, one containing the indispensable *Mater Dolorosa* in a stiff black brocade dress with glassy eyes staring out of her life-size doll's face; the other, Christ on the *via crucis* as described in the church at Torre Cardela, with long soft brown hair falling round His velvet-robed shoulders.

The morning was fresh and when I returned to the *posada* for breakfast I found the dining-room shutters were closed to keep out the cold: but the children of the *pueblo* had collected outside to see me. At intervals they pushed open the shutters and I got up and shut them again. Then one of the boys climbed up the iron bars on the outside of the window and pushed open two little flaps at the top of the shutters. These proved impossible to latch and as soon as I shut them the boy would push them open again and shout to the inquisitive crowds below him: 'The woman eats! The woman reads! The woman writes!' This was surely a worse intrusion on one's privacy than is suffered by royalty? For I believe that even the Queen is not stared at during breakfast. Sometimes I got up, waved my arms and screamed 'Go away!' when my persecutor would disappear for a split second only to pop up again like a jack-in-a-box: 'The woman speaks!'

There was a school inspector staying in the *posada*. He seemed shy, and sat at a narrow table against the wall. He took no part in the battle raging between me and the children and sat unperturbed munching his breakfast of bread and sausage, which he ate off the point of his knife. His food had been wrapped in brown paper and he had taken it out of what appeared to be a pillow-case, his sole travelling bag. His shyness was infectious but at last I summoned up the courage to start a conversation and got him to help me with my verbs. He told me he had come by car to Don Diego from Guadix, and having inspected the four schools there was proceeding on a donkey to the next *pueblo* along the valley.

The *posada* in Don Diego is not a cave-dwelling but a structural building in a row of whitewashed houses. There are two or three such streets in the village, one of them containing a general stores and a café, and another the church. In the small grey hills round the back of the village are the caves. The ground-plan of the *posada* consists of an oblong covered cobbled yard acting as a sort of narthex to the great dark stable beyond it. At one end of this narthex is a tiny kitchen with the usual open fire, and a windowless bedroom occupied by the landlord and his family, and at the other end the dining-room and the stone staircase leading up to the two guest bedrooms and a whole row of store-rooms leading one into the other and full of grain and vegetables and fruit: grapes and tomatoes hang drying along the beams. From all the upper windows of the inn and the other houses hang strings of scarlet pimientos.

After breakfast my landlord, Rosendo Fernando Corall, led me into the mysterious depths of the stable and showed me a swelling on the Marquesa's barrel which had come up in the night. He said it was caused by the girth having been done up too tight. I suggested hot fomentations, but he said cold water was best and he went and fetched some in an enamel basin and threw it, a little at a time, over the affected part. He was proved right as it gradually subsided with regular treatment until by the time I left Don Diego three days later it had completely disappeared.

Rosendo loved animals and took a great pride in his mule which stood near to the Marquesa and was in lovely condition. Beside the usual *paja y cebada* he cut luscious bundles of lucerne for it from his own plot of ground. There was also a well-cared-for white donkey mare and her yearling foal in a loose-box off the main stable, which belonged to his father-in-law. It is wrong to say that Spaniards are unkind to animals. I do not intend to go into the morality of bull-fighting. I simply wish to state that in their day-to-day relationships with domestic animals they are both kind and knowledgeable. You do sometimes see harness galls on mules and donkeys and pack-horses but these are treated with a special lotion known to every muleteer and the offending breast-plate or breeching is left off until the sore is healed. After all, those of us who hunt or race or show-jump in England cannot avoid sometimes giving our horses and ponies bowed tendons, sprained shoulders, sore mouths and even sore backs, therefore we are not in a position to preach to other people. And if the various anti-sport societies succeed in stopping sport then our horses and ponies will become largely extinct and those that remain will be desperately bored spoilt pets. The happy horse is the working horse: fair work, fair food and fair rest, and that is what most Spanish animals get. With regard to deliberate cruelty provoked by anger or by sexual aberration this is alas common to all peoples owing to the beastliness of man, and is by no means peculiar to Spaniards.

Rosendo said he would clean my tack and rub hog's lard into the girth to soften it. Apart from her lump, the mare was due for a full day's rest, so I decided to go for a walk in the *vega* which turned out to be a garden of paradise in the midst of the infernal regions. The little river Fardes runs through a narrow channel in a wide stony bed on the far side of the ravine and between it and Don Diego there is a strip of fertile land planted with peach and almond and pomegranate and fig and olive trees; close to the river there are several plantations of young poplars, their leaves shimmering gold in autumn glory. I managed to dodge the many children who seemed never to go to school in Spain and who started to follow me, and sat against an olive tree and did my homework for three hours on end. Suddenly half the olives fell off the tree, I shook it so with my laughter. I had got to one of those good coarse passages of Cervantean lavatory humour which was so applicable to loo-life at a *posada* that I split my sides reading it.

I asked Carmen Corall Martinez, my landlady, if I could have *jamón* for luncheon so we went together to a neighbour's house and bought a few slices which were then fried for me. After lunch I went to the village shop to buy myself a *navaja*, a jack-knife, which everybody carries in Andalusia. In the good old days it was useful for sticking into your enemy as well as into your meat: from now on I found mine invaluable for scraping my boots, picking out the mare's feet and for eating off. The shop was well stocked with barley, flour, sugar, loops of sausage hanging from the beams, socks, canvas shoes and the sort of rope-soled sandals I had seen Fernando go to work in at Moclín. There appeared to be no tinned food. I bought a very nice comb as mine was broken, some chocolate, Marie biscuits (which seemed to be the only species obtainable anywhere) and half a kilo of boiled sweets for the children who were pressing into the shop to see exactly what I was buying. Another customer apologised to me for their behaviour, saying they were '*sin educación*'. I said that perhaps they did not see many foreigners. He told me that I was the first English person to come to Don Diego in living memory. This is the marvellous thing about rural Spain: the country roads are, thank God, sufficiently bad and full of hazards, such as potholes and fords, to deter the motorist; the smaller *pueblos*, though beautiful and unspoilt, contain no good pictures or outstanding architecture to attract culture-vultures, so that you may ride or walk for literally hundreds of miles without meeting anyone but Spaniards provided that you steer clear of the tourist centres.

I left the shop surrounded by children clamouring for sweets which I distributed as fairly as possible. I asked them to take me to see their caves and we spent the next hour or so exploring them. I learnt the following facts from the inhabitants: that though troglodyte colonies have existed for hundreds (probably thousands) of years in this great ravine running northwards from Guadix (the famous trog-town)* to the valley of the Guadalquivir, a distance of some eighty miles, caves are still being excavated to-day for families to live in. The hills out of which they are dug are of clay (argillaceous sandstone) and it takes two men approximately six weeks to cut out a four-roomed dwelling, one doing the hacking, the other wheeling the earth away. All the ceilings must be coved to carry the weight of the hill above them. The floors are often tiled and the walls are always whitewashed annually

* Brenan: *op. cit.*, ch. xiv.

just as in the structural houses. More often than not the façade is stone-faced and whitewashed and there is a window in each of the front rooms with no glass in it, but iron bars to exclude thieves, not draughts. Further ventilation is provided by the tall wide round chimney which sticks so oddly out of the top of the little hill.

In Don Diego you can buy a ready-excavated cave-house, with electricity laid on, for £90 to £120 according to its condition and the number of rooms you require. Should you want to dig out a new one you do not have to pay rent to anybody for your bit of hill. Formerly it was the custom to pay a chicken a year to the lord of the village, Don Diego, by whose name the *pueblo* is still locally known though it is different from the one which appears on the map. To either side of your cave you can cut out hen-houses and stables and sties, according to the requirements of your livestock. There are always some bushes handy on which to hang your washing.

I was asked into the living-room of several caves, each one of which was as clean as a new pin and much more spacious and comfortable than those in some of the ordinary houses and inns I had seen. The cooking facilities were identical: a large open hooded fireplace burning twigs and banked up *paja*. I would like above all to make it clear that the word 'cave' is not synonymous with 'slum' as some people in England seem to think. There are poor people and better-off people and some quite well-to-do people living in troglodyte colonies just as in any of our council house estates; and most of the families living in them are of Spanish and not gypsy blood. In point of fact I only saw two gypsies in Don Diego.

The trog children are clean and well-dressed in brightly coloured hand-knitted jerseys and home-made skirts or trousers. They cannot afford the luxury of expensive shoes but wear rope-soled canvas ones or sandals. I saw no signs of rickety legs and they have lovely skins and beautiful teeth. Their every gastronomic whim is not catered for and no ice-cream van drives past their caves playing an irritating theme-tune on bells. No cake shop tempts them with cardboard éclairs stuffed with mock cream and they have no pocket money with which to buy sweets. But theirs is not the starvation-level poverty of the east: their daily diet of *cocidos* and *pucheros* and excellent bread, and fresh fruit, and occasional eggs and fish, together with nine months' sunshine in every year turns them into beautiful specimens of humanity and they doubtless have tougher bodies and better teeth than a lot of over-indulged children in our welfare state.

I returned to the *posada* laden with pomegranates and grapes from my trog hosts. The school inspector had gone and the only guest was a tinker boy who looked about fifteen and who rode from village to village on his donkey mending frying-pans and *ollas*. He was sitting on his pack-saddle in the narthex eating black pudding off his *navaja*. It was a cold evening and an icy wind blew in through all the cracks of the dining-room shutters, so I went and sat in the little kitchen where there was actually glass in the narrow window, though the wind managed to find a way in through the space between the wooden frame and the wall. Carmen was sitting on a low chair by the fire feeding cereal to her little eight-month-old Rhesus baby, Juan Jesús, with a spoon. Her daughter Pilar (named after the much-venerated Virgen del Pilar at Saragossa) was a healthy girl of six and had been born a normal baby. Her next two children died soon after birth because Carmen was a Rhesus negative (so-called because the blood factor was first discovered in the Rhesus monkey) with antibodies which destroyed the red corpuscles in the infant's blood-stream. Her fourth baby was born in Granada hospital and within an hour of birth the infant was stretched out on splints in the form of a cross to help the lungs expand. A polythene two-way syringe was carefully inserted into the artery of the umbilical cord and the blood gradually drawn out of the tiny body. Meanwhile the same quantity of fresh blood from the hospital bank was pumped in through the other channel of the syringe, about two pints in all. There is now a national health service in Spain, each person paying 40 *pesetas* a month (5/–), so that all Carmen's treatment was free.

I sat and wrote letters at a small table against the wall in which was a drawer containing stale bread for *migas*, a soup made of garlic and breadcrumbs fried in olive oil with water added. The handsome old grandpa was there and at 9.30 p.m. we all had supper of *cocido* and bread: my word, chickpeas are good when you are hungry! In addition to the usual fuel Carmen burnt a few maize husks and fir-cones on her open fire and I noticed some pine brushwood in reserve to start off an extra large *olla*. In one corner of the hearth there was a small square iron boiling stove into the bottom of which red-hot embers could be inserted and with a few fir-cones on top of them a quick and efficient heat could be obtained.

After supper Carmen took me, at my special request, to call on one of the village schoolmistresses, Doña Encarnacion, who lived two doors away. She and her husband and brother-in-law and her little boy of four, Antonito, were sitting round their cosy-table in a small room so that there was a nice warm fug. They welcomed me to the table. I explained that I was a catechist in my own *pueblo*, a member of *Las catequistas de nuestra Señora*, and that I would be most interested to attend one of her classes. She said she would be delighted and that the next one would be on Saturday afternoon and would consist of an exposition of the Sunday Gospel. She was an enchanting person, I should say in her middle thirties, breathing out goodness and happiness and enthusiasm like so many of her kind. Her husband, who worked their little bit of land, obviously adored her and his little son, and without wishing to be mawkish, I must say that they struck me as a living example of the Holy Family, but with the wireless always on. They invited me to come in whenever I wanted to read or write, knowing how cold the *posada* could be.

Later, while heating some water for my bottle in a small saucepan with no lid, on Carmen's iron stove, I observed a kettle with a folding handle up on a shelf and asked if I could use that but was told it was a coffee-pot.

Friday, November 10

We threw more cold water at the Marquesa's lump in the morning and I decided to exercise her bareback so as to give it every chance of going down. We forded the stream below the village where the animals water and the women wash, then crossed the *vega* to the river Fardes and followed its course upsteam towards Guadix, crossing and recrossing it at the many fords. Along the dry part of the river-bed there was a sand path used apparently exclusively by goats judging by the droppings (developing an eye for droppings is an essential accomplishment in cross-country riding in Spain). When these led down to the channel of rushing water and out again on the far side, you knew it was safe to cross.

About three miles downstream among the shimmering golden poplars on either bank, we came to a formidable black Mantegna precipice to the left beyond which it was impossible to pass. So we cut across the now narrow *vega* to the stony road which leads from Don Diego to Guadix. As we approached the *pueblo* I saw two mules tied up outside a solitary cave-dwelling with a whitewashed stone façade. Out came an old man and his beautiful daughter so I asked if I could photograph them. I was, of course, asked in, the old man tying up the mare with the mules. I was given an extra juicy pomegranate to eat, sitting by the open fire. There were two little girls playing on the floor so I asked if they were the young woman's but she said no, their mother was dead so she was living here with her father and housekeeping for the caveholder and his children. There were four rooms in the cave, each of the two front ones (the living-room and best bedroom) having a window with a *reja* (iron bars) but no glass, and two bedrooms burrowed deep into the hill at the back. Curtains took the place of doors. I was shown a photograph hanging on the wall and covered with a piece of cloth. This was lifted up to reveal the face of a good-looking young man. It was the woman's first cousin who, she told me, had been murdered in 1952 by another man. I asked was it over a girl? But she said no, it was *'por nada'* (for nothing). So I supposed it was the result of one of those displays of Latin temperament when knives are drawn which Ford describes as being so common in his time. We returned to the table and she told me of her nephew aged ten who was studying at the seminary school at Guadix and of how good the local *cura* had been to him. She was called Caridad.

That evening I rode a little way along the mule-track in the opposite direction and found a bank of delicious grass along the side of an irrigation canal where the Marquesa stuffed herself full. She thought of very little else but food and would go on grazing for much longer at a time than an English horse. I think this was because the grass was much shorter in this arid land so it took her longer to get it. Anyway it was a blessing never to have to bother to tie her up, and to know that for as long as I continued to do my homework on *Don Quixote* she would continue to guzzle at her grass. I could find no suitable place for mounting without the saddle when the time came to go home. Some inquisitive boys from an isolated cave above me were vastly amused at my unsuccessful attempts. In the end I had to invoke the aid of a passing muleteer who gave me a professional leg-up. He did not laugh but took it as a matter of course to help an elderly lady in distress. How far from being *sin educación* are these noble Andalusians!

After supper of fried eggs and melon I went round and spent the evening with Doña Encarna and her family and at her request, attempted to tell her the story of my conversion to Catholicism.

It was raining and icy cold when I went to bed at midnight so I slept in all my underclothes with pyjamas on the top of them and two jerseys pulled over the pyjamas.

SATURDAY, NOVEMBER 11

We rode along the same track as the night before but went further. We had to cross a tiny bridge over a narrow irrigation channel and nothing on earth would make the Marquesa do it. I got off and tried to lead her over: I coaxed, I threatened, I called her a cow, a *mulo*, but nothing would budge her. Then I broke all pony club rules and tied her up by the reins—that is to say I fixed a long piece of cord to the reins the other end of which I tied to a thorn bush on the far side of the minute bridge. I then went round to her rear and slapped her hard on the quarters (which hurt me much more than her) shouting loudly. Very dignified, she took a couple of steps back and broke both cheek pieces of her bridle. How often I have ticked off children for tying up their ponies by the reins!

She won that round but I was more than ever determined to get us both over the canal because, like the proverbial chicken, I wanted to see what was on the other side. I carried half the bridle with the bit and reins in one hand and led the mare with the other, having tied the cord to the noseband. Fifty yards further on there was another wider bridge over which the maddening creature followed me like a lamb though it meant sitting on her haunches and sliding down a prodigiously steep bank on the far side. I managed to mount off the bottom of this bank and found the Marquesa was every bit as easy to control without a bit as with one, because all Spanish horses neck-rein and the cord would turn her this way or that and a pull on it with a 'Brrrrrr' would stop her.

I dismounted a mile further on by a rushing mountain stream and mugged up my Spanish catechism (*primer grado*) while the Marquesa had her elevenses which she so little deserved.

After luncheon I went round to the school which consisted of a single oblong room on the first floor of Doña Encarna's house. Counted thirty-seven little girls, after the last late-comer had sat down at her small blue desk, aged from six to ten years. There was only one tall narrow window (with glass) in the classroom, behind the teacher's desk, and I thought how far better this plan was for concentration than the distracting glass walls of our modern English schools. When doing a W.E.A. course in one of them the year before I spent most of the time looking across to a recreation room were the members of the local youth club were playing ping-pong. How could I be expected to fix my mind on medieval history?

Before starting the lesson we all stood up and said together the *oración de la entrada:*

'Enlighten our understanding O Lord and move our will so that with attention and diligence we will learn more easily the things which are taught us for our spiritual and temporal good. We pray this for the sake of Our Lord Jesus Christ. Amen.'

There followed three Hail Mary's, after which Doña Encarna read out slowly and clearly the Parable of the Wheat and the Tares. She then explained to the little girls exactly what a parable was and the inner meaning of this one and how the teaching contained in it applied just as

51

much to our time as to the time when Our Lord lived in Palestine. I hoped so much that Don Jorge Borrow, with his passionate love of the Gospel, was listening with joy to this lesson.

While it was going on an elderly lady dressed entirely in black sat on a low chair by the window sewing, while little Antonito, Doña Encarna's four-year-old son, kept running in and out wanting this and that. The discipline was excellent and the children took no notice of him, even when he went up and flung his arms round a chubby little girl who kept her eyes solemnly fixed on the *Maestra*.

Then followed some reading practice and arithmetic during which naughty little Antonito, fed up by his failure to attract the attention of the well-disciplined pupils, climbed up onto a desk and started to do his own version of *flamenco* dancing. The *Maestra*, her patience at an end, left the blackboard and carried him out to his father in the kitchen next door.

At four o'clock we all said the five glorious mysteries of the Rosary together, it being Saturday, the day of the week specially dedicated to Our Lady. Then the children recited the *oración de la salida*.

'We give Thee thanks O Lord, for having helped us with Thy light and we implore Thee to continue giving us Thy divine help, so that those things which we have learnt may further our spiritual and temporal good; we pray this for the sake of Jesus Christ Our Lord. Amen.'

SUNDAY, NOVEMBER 12

I went to the first Mass at 7 a.m. because I woke up very early. It was fairly well attended by women who sat on the right of the aisle, the few men sitting on the left. The *cura* preached for twenty-five minutes on the Parable of the Wheat and the Tares and I was delighted to understand so much of it thanks to having been well prepared by Doña Encarna. I reflected on how much easier it is to drive home the teaching of Our Lord in rural Spain where Biblical methods of agriculture are still practised, than in England where everything is mechanised and you have to explain what a reaper is as opposed to a combine harvester. I decided to go to the second Mass at 10 a.m. to hear the sermon over again. This was well attended by a lot of women and children, among them naughty little Antonito and his Mama, and a fair proportion of men. But I was much distracted by thinking about the chicken I had asked Carmen to kill for my Sunday luncheon. It is dreadful how often my thoughts stray to cooking when in church. I may start off with the best *intention* to hear Mass well, but my *attention* is quite another thing and soon wanders off into recipes and menu-planning until recalled by the Sanctus bell.

After the second Mass I went along to Doña Encarna's house to write letters in the schoolroom which was both light and warm because of the glass in the window. Meanwhile she and her husband were preparing their Sunday lunch in the kitchen next door. This consisted of a thick pancake made without eggs or milk but simply with flour, water and olive oil beaten together and fried over the open fire in the largest iron frying-pan I have ever seen. It must have measured at least eighteen inches in diameter. Señor Barros sat on a low chair over the fire and when the great moment of tossing arrived, he got up, took hold of the long pan handle with both hands, threw up and caught the gigantic crêpe on its top side, and returned the pan to the fire where the cooking process continued for a further ten minutes. When it was ready Doña Encarna begged me to have a little. She said it was called *miga* (which actually means crumb) and that most people in Don Diego would be eating it to-day because it was a favourite cold weather dish. I could not help thinking of all the roast Sunday joints on the tables of England. We sat round and ate the pancake straight out of the pan with some little white grapes, the traditional accompaniment. It was excellent, but I felt very ashamed returning to the *posada* afterwards to devour my chicken in solitary state. It had only been killed that morning as poultry and meat is never hung in Andalusia even in cold weather, so it was rather tough: but any sort of meat was a treat after a week of vegetable soups and stews. I was given a leg and wing and the liver, heart, gizzard and kidneys, the three last delicacies being very much appreciated by my good friends the cats. Then I had a tin of the local peaches. A feast fit for a Queen.

After luncheon I went across to Señora Lola, the Balzacian character who provides the local *cura* with his main meals. I wanted to ask him if he would like me to play the harmonium for Benediction. But he had finished his lunch and left the cave. Did he too have *miga*? Señora Lola invited me in for a gossip and piled her fire high with maize husks which provided a nice blaze. We sat in rocking-chairs on either side of the fire and you got the sensation of being in a very nice sitting-room in an ordinary house. Neighbours kept dropping in for a few minutes and when they left more came. I practised the verbs I had learnt from the school inspector with great success and told them all about foxhunting.

I decided to give a dinner-party for Doña Encarna and her family at my *posada*, so asked my landlady to get a bottle of *vino tinto* and make us a *tortilla* apiece. Then I went and invited the schoolmistress who beamed all over and thanked me profusely. The time fixed was 8.30 p.m.

Doña Encarna and her husband, Señor Barros, his brother, and little Antonito arrived at 8.20 but Carmen mistook the time and we did not get our dinner until 9.15. I racked my brains as to how best I could entertain my

guests, limited as were my powers of conversation. Finally
I hit on drawing, an art for which I have singularly little
talent, having failed twice to get my Girl Guide's artist's
badge. But my *burros* and *caballos* and even a *cocodrilo* kept
Antonito vastly amused. Then I became more ambitious
and drew St George and the Dragon and St James and
the Moor until at last a series of vast *tortillas* appeared
and a bottle of wine with a plastic straw through the cork
which we passed round and drank as from a *porrón*. Slices
of melon completed the menu.

While we were eating two girls came in and said the
Juez (Justice of the Peace) wanted to meet me before I
left, he had not been able to invite me to his house before
owing to illness. So when we had finished eating, Señor
Barros kindly offered to take me down to the house in
the lower half of the *pueblo*. The old gentleman was sitting
at his cosy-table surrounded by his family and I told him
as much as I could about my riding tour and about
England and foxhunting. Then I said how sorry I was to
find that nobody in Andalusian *pueblos* played the guitar
any more.

'But,' I said, 'many of you sing *cante jondo* very beautifully.'

'Yes, Fernando does,' came a chorus from the cosy-
table.

'No, no, no,' protested the young man on my right.

'I suppose you only sing when you are drunk,' I said.
This feeble joke, my first in Spanish, brought the house
down.

We returned to Doña Encarna's house because it was
warmer than the *posada*, and she showed me her bedroom
with an almost life-size figure of the infant Jesus in a crib
on her dressing-table. Such figures are not only brought
out at Christmas as they are in England, but seem to be a
permanent feature in many Spanish households. We then
talked about education and she told me that owing to the

shortage of teachers and accommodation most of the schools were run in two sessions, the morning one being for one group and the afternoon for another. This explains why there are always children playing in the *pueblos*, even during school hours. She also said that two new school buildings were under construction in Don Diego and that when they were finished four more teachers would be sent to the village so that all the children would soon be able to attend the full school day. We finally exchanged addresses and promised to write to one another and parted with much affection, the *Maestra* giving me a copy of the life of St John of God as a farewell gift.

MONDAY, NOVEMBER 13

I had arranged for Juan, my landlady's first cousin, to guide me out of the infernal regions as there were no roads leading to my next port of call: only a labyrinth of mule-tracks and I knew I would never find the right one to lead me over the pale grey sierras on the far side of the canyon. When Juan had first called at the *posada* two days previously to fix terms, he wore his working clothes and had three days' growth of beard on his chin. So I simply did not recognise him until he came up and told me we ought to start in half an hour. He wore a neat blue suit and a grey homburg hat and had evidently just emerged from the barber's. He was a smallholder and had a nice, stocky black 13 hands 2-in. pony which he rode in an *aparejo*, the mattress-like pack-saddle used for all pack-animals in Spain, and a headcollar with only a rope to guide it by.

I think the whole *pueblo* was there to see us off, including a great crowd of exceptionally beautiful and healthy-looking children. As usual my landlord had to fetch a chair before I could climb up onto the Marquesa and as usual everyone was too nice to laugh. I made my custom-

ary royal exit, this time enhanced by my mounted attendant Juan, and I shouted '*Adios! Adios!*' while Doña
Encarna and all the children shouted back '*Vaya Usted
con Dio-o-o-o-o.*'

We set off along the same track through the garden of
paradise as that which led to my scene with the Marquesa,
only Juan knew of an alternative path which led over a
wide bridge. Further on we turned right across the valley,
riding through peach plantations, then through wilder
country with casuarina trees and bamboo and oleander,
to the banks of the river Guadiana Menor which we
forded easily in spite of Juan's fears that it might be too
deep after the recent rains. I put my feet up on either side
of the Marquesa's shoulders and reached the further bank
without getting wet.

We then rode along a soft grey track which led up into
the bare beautifully modelled clay hills of Giotto's frescoes. As we got higher there was an ever wider view of
the river valley below and the interminable grey sierras
beyond it. This sort of landscape gives you an insight
into Eternity: it is so vast and so beautiful and so still
that you would like it to go on for ever.

Once out of the infernal regions we rode across a plain
where flocks of sheep grazed on invisible grass. We
passed a boy about eight years old riding a nice grey
pony with a black mane and tail in a string halter with
just a blanket thrown over its back. He was carrying a
large basket of cabbages and had the natural seat of the
born horseman. Then we came to some low grey hills
covered with small round towers which turned out to be
the chimneys of another trog colony. When I looked
closer I could see some very superior cave-dwellings with
front rooms of whitewashed stone built against the hill
with strings of red peppers hanging from them, and
brightly coloured shirts and frocks drying on the bushes
near the doors. The Marquesa was going very short and

I found a stone lodged in her off-fore foot which neither Juan nor I could dislodge with our *navajas*, so I led her the remaining half-mile to the *posada* in Cuevas del Campo where a hammer and pincers had to be produced to remove it. The animals then went up a very steep step into the stable and were fed *cebada y paja* while I went to explore the *pueblo*.

There was one long main street with a church half-way up it. Most of the houses here were free-standing but some of them were built against the hill behind them with caves forming the back rooms. On either side of this main street there were grey hills riddled with troglodyte dwellings, far more than at Don Diego but in a less romantic setting. I spoke to the *cura* who was standing outside his little church and asked if he minded if I went into it in jodhpurs. Discovered that he spoke French rather better than I did Spanish so we conversed in that language. He very kindly took me into the church himself and explained that it was only thirty years old as Cuevas had grown to its present size of four thousand inhabitants during the past half century. The building was whitewashed both inside and out and had pointed windows and a nice little tower that blended well with its surroundings. To the right of the high altar a door led into his presbytery where there was a smart Hispano-Olivetti typewriter on the desk. He offered me a glass of brandy which I felt ungrateful at refusing but I just cannot swallow spirits unless pushed by acute pain. So I had a large glass of refreshing cold water while we talked of the coming Ecumenical Council and the problems connected with reunion. He offered me lunch but Juan was waiting to have it with me at the *posada* so back I went.

I had brought the remains of my Sunday chicken along in a small cardboard box and Juan and I set to at a cosy table, for some inexplicable reason in a bedroom on the first floor. It was all quite proper because we were sur-

rounded by the landlord and his family and several of
their friends, including a poor little crippled boy who
dragged himself about the floor on his hands because his
legs were paralysed. Eating tough cockerel with nothing
but a jack-knife and your fingers before an admiring
audience is a typical ordeal to which you must get accustomed when touring in rural Spain. Our landlady
provided bread, tomatoes, melon and pomegranates and
having eaten all we wanted I settled the account, including
Juan's keep for the night and extra *cebada* for the pony.
He could perfectly well have returned to Don Diego that
afternoon (a three-hour ride) but I had originally agreed
to pay a night's keep at Cuevas for him; he had five
children and a sick wife, so I was delighted to treat him
to a night out.

At four o'clock I set off on my own, along the straight
flat unmetalled road to Pozo Alcón, eleven kilometres
away. Suddenly a young man with a coal-black bristly
face galloped past me sitting sideways on a donkey,
chasing his leading donkey which had gone on ahead
towards home while its master had stopped to have a
drink in Cuevas. Such an extraordinary feat of balance
I have never seen outside a circus. When he finally drew
halter rope (as opposed to rein) he shouted back at me
that he would accompany me to Pozo which was an appal-
ling bore as I longed to be alone for a bit. So we rode
along together while he ate his lunch: an enormous
quantity of bread and *raw* fish which he slit open with his
navaja, removing the guts with his little finger which
seemed to me an unnecessary refinement. He of course
offered to share his meal but I protested, as politely as
I could, that I had only just had lunch at the *posada*: I was,
however, delighted to accept some walnuts and dried figs
which he next produced out of a grimy pocket.

As we rode along he told me he was a coal merchant
and had just delivered some coal to Cuevas. As I was a

traveller I probably did not want to buy any coal. But would I like to buy some of his excellent home-cured *jamón* to take with me? Or perhaps his leading donkey to carry my belongings? I said that everything fitted very well into my *alforjas* and that the Marquesa was well able to carry them as well as me. This was a social occasion on which I badly needed my lost *bota*: Juan had one and I had had to drink out of it repeatedly on our morning ride for the sake of etiquette.

The coal merchant now proceeded to cross-question me as to how much I had paid at this and that *posada*, how much I had paid Juan, etc. (I quoted lower figures all the time), till I got so bored that I asked him to sing in order to stop him talking.

'Give me a hundred *pesetas*.'

'No—ten.'

'A hundred.'

Exasperated, I started to sing myself and treated him to all three verses of the *Lorelei* in German, one of my set pieces. All I got for this was to be told how poor he was as he pointed to his knees sticking through his trousers. In self-defence I said I would give him twenty-five *pesetas* if he would sing to me for the rest of the journey.

'Give me a hundred *pesetas*!'

I handed him a twenty-five *peseta* piece which he could not resist and he started to sing *cante jondo* very well indeed. But not for long.

'*¡Me da cien peseta!*' he shouted threateningly, barring the Marquesa's path with his sweet little *burro*.

'I go alone to Pozo!' I shouted back as I dug the iron points of my Moorish stirrups into the Marquesa's sides so that we set off at a smart canter along the soft sandy side of the road, *alforjas* flapping madly. I could hear little tiny galloping feet pursuing me, but not for long, the Marquesa's long stride soon outdistanced the donkeys, though I kept her cantering for at least a mile to put a

comfortable distance between me and the nearest thing
I ever got to a bandit.

Up till now I had felt too self-conscious to say 'May
you go with God!' to people I met or took leave of; but
speed gave me courage and I shouted: '¡*Vaya usted con
Dio-o-o-o-o!*' at the top of my voice to everyone we passed.
It was very exhilarating.

Pozo Alcón is a large *pueblo* of 12,000 inhabitants with
three doctors and three priests. It has a big cement factory
and an olive oil refinery. About fifty men are at present
employed in building a dam nine kilometres away which
will be used for electricity and for irrigation.

The *posada* to which I was directed had a very grand-
sounding name: '*Parador del Carmen. Camas y Comidas*'
(beds and meals) 'GARAGE'. I led the Marquesa through
the usual covered cobbled yard into the garage which was
full of mules, but I was told that they were tied up there
temporarily while their masters were drinking at the bar,
and that the real stable was beyond. My landlord's eldest
son, a smiling boy of sixteen, delightedly removed the
saddle for me and fetched some *cebada*, and during the
two days I spent in this inn he was the mare's constant
attendant, taking her out to water, seeing she had a con-
tinual supply of *paja* and saddling and unsaddling her.
The corn feeds I always gave myself.

I had a single bedroom with a narrow window facing
north which actually had some glass in it. But as the top
pane was half out and the shutters did not shut properly and
the *pueblo* stood on a high plain at the foot of the Sierra del
Pozo with an icy wind blowing off it, the room was extremely cold and draughty. I unpacked my saddle-bags to
find that my nice Dayella pyjamas had been jolted out in
my flight. So the coal boy had won after all—having picked
up a prize worth at least three hundred *pesetas*! Perhaps
he would wear the striped legs on his rounds in place
of the torn pants with which he failed to arouse my pity?

Noah's Ark

Opposite my bedroom there was a loo with the most ingenious plan for embarrassing the occupant which I have yet come across: it was L-shaped and the door was too big for its frame to shut properly. In the upper half there should have been four panes of frosted glass but one of them was missing so that any passer-by could look right in. When you slammed the door from the inside it stuck to its jambs for half a minute then burst open with a triumphant squeak. Impossible to reach round the angle of the wall to shut it again.

Having had no time to myself on the road all day and supper not being for another four hours, I sat in my bed with two pairs of socks on, two jerseys and my overcoat and wrote some letters. But the snow-laden wind blew into my bones so I got up and went to evening devotions. Surprised to hear '*Dios te salve Maria*' coming through a loud-speaker onto the plaza outside the church. This was the priest speaking through a mike as he led the congregation in the recitation of the Rosary from the pulpit. Afterwards I asked him what time Mass would be as the *posada* was ten minutes' walk away and I might not hear the three bells. He said 'Eight-thirty, no eight forty-five, no nine o'clock *mas seguro.*'

Back from evening devotions I went to the stable to give the Marquesa her supper but could not open the door for the sheep which were leaning against it. Eventually forced my way in and fell flat across a fat ewe. She smelt deliciously of lanoline. When I finally got to the Marquesa there was another ewe lying on the chopped straw in her manger. She looked so cosy that I could not bear to dislodge her, so I moved the mare down a peg. Besides the sheep there were several large pigs, a string of nine mules, five donkeys, seven goats, two ponies, two white turkeys and a lot of chickens in the stable which resembled Noah's Ark. As I left I caught the naughty Marquesa directing a sly kick at one of the poor pigs.

Party nerves

When I went along to the dining-room for supper my
nerve nearly failed me: there were no less than seven men
sitting at an outsize cosy-table eating saffron-coloured
fish soup. I got the same sort of sinking feeling as I did
thirty years ago before going into a deb's dinner-party.
But now, as then, I had to go through with it so I sat
down between an electrician working on the dam with
the face of a Byzantine Saint, and a jovial round-faced pig
dealer who had been buying pigs at the market and had
seen and greatly admired my mare.

'*Que buena jaca*' (What a good hack!) he said, little
knowing that the Marquesa was doing her best to maim
his purchases.

I asked him if he had any horses of his own. He told
me he had a farm near Pozo and used to keep two horses
on it but they ate so much he sold them. Now he only
keeps mules for farm work.

Maria, the seventeen-year-old girl who waited on us,
had flashing black eyes and flirted outrageously with the
customers. Afterwards while sitting in the kitchen waiting to fill my hot-water bottle I met my host and hostess
and their nine children. She did all the *posada* cooking
while the children played in and out of the kitchen and
the garage and the stables. Talked to a dam engineer and
his wife who had not been at my supper table. They came
from Madrid and she was lamenting her fate at being
stuck in this remote provincial town. I suggested that
she ought to buy a horse and explore the surrounding
sierras but she did not seem to think it a good idea.

In this large *posada* the cooking is not done on an open
fire but at a tiled charcoal stove all along one wall. But
even here there was no oven, so that the menus were
confined to fried foods and stews.

Pyjamaless, I went to bed in two sets of underclothes,
including a lovely long pair of pants I bought at Malaga,
my two jerseys and two extra blankets provided by Maria;

with a very hot hot-water bottle and my overcoat on top
of the lot, I really was warm at last.

Only the French know how to deal with St Antony so
I dozed off reciting . . .

> '*Saint Antoine de Padou*
> *Grand cocain, grand voleur, grand filou*
> *Qui connaissez tous les p'tits trous*
> *Rendez nous c'qui n'est pas a vous!*'

which had made him cough up so much for me in the
past. But in my heart of hearts I felt that there was nothing
he could do about my Dayella pyjamas.

TUESDAY, NOVEMBER 14

I went to Mass at 9 (*mas seguro* at that hour the priest had
said) to find that the Gospel was half finished. Oh! Mass
times are the most exasperating of all the *cosas de España*!
Excellent espresso coffee from the *posada* bar for breakfast, after which I went along to the hairdresser, having
made an appointment the previous evening. I was now
three-quarters of an hour late but the Señora had not even
put the water on to heat, I was so punctual according to
her ideas. The 'salon' was the small living-room in a small
house in a side street. There was no window at all, so the
front door had to be left open to let in light to aid the
low-watt electric bulb. Eventually a saucepan of hot water
was carried in from the next room and I was subjected to
the following ordeal:

1. A very large shallow basin was placed in the circular frame of a chair without a seat.
2. I knelt on a cushion in front of it and bowed my
head as for decapitation.
3. An icy snow-laden wind blew in onto my legs.
4. The basin was part filled with hot water from the

saucepan and cold water from a bucket by Natividad, the
Señora's daughter.

5. My head was thoroughly washed and rinsed in two
waters while the hairdresser told me the sad story of her
life: how her husband had walked out on her when her
baby was still unborn; how he had never been heard of
since, so that Natividad had never seen her father; how
she had gone to stay with an aunt in Alicante for six
months to learn her trade. While she first cut and then
set my hair, her little girl shivered in a cotton frock and
cardigan and handed out the rollers. Finally, I was put
under a gloriously warm modern electric drier while
Natividad sat close beside me eating her breakfast (11 a.m.)
of dry bread and nut milk chocolate.

The hairdresser charged me fifteen *pesetas* for my wash,
cut and set—under two shillings. I was horrified and gave
her twenty-five for which she was touchingly grateful.
I then decided to go along to the saddlers to get some
extra straps put on the flaps of my saddle-bags. Nothing
shuts properly in Spain: neither windows nor shutters nor
alforjas nor loo doors. Natividad returned to the *posada*
with me and we fetched the bags and the bridle (which
had been temporarily stitched with esparto thread by my
landlord at Don Diego) and she took me along to the
main street of Pozo which leads uphill to the church and
where I had already noticed a great variety of shops:
grocers, ironmongers, a clock shop, two chemists, cloth
merchants and a covered municipal market where you
could buy fish and meat and vegetables and fruit and
groceries. We went into the saddler's shop which was
hung with beautiful samples of his craft: embroidered
saddle-cloths and bags, breastplates and breechings and
lovely shocking pink and scarlet *burro* bridles. I explained
about the cheek pieces of the Marquesa's bridle and
showed the saddler where I wanted him to sew on extra
straps and buckles to prevent my losing any more treasures

out of my *alforjas*. I also bought a rope halter for tying the Marquesa up at night. Up till now she had only had a bit of string round her neck.

Lunch at 2 p.m. consisted of very good *cocido*, a French omelette and tinned peaches. My only companions were a good-looking young officer in the Civil Guard, and a furniture maker from Baeza who said he was planning to go to Switzerland to practise his trade as he had some friends there to go to and could earn more money. He told me he was not married though he looked about thirty years old, so I advised him to get a pretty Swiss bride.

When the evening light was just right for photography I walked up to the winding hilly streets at the top of the town and as I was wandering about taking picturesque groups of women sitting knitting and sewing outside their houses, a young woman came up to me and asked if I had lost anything on the road yesterday. Astonished, I followed her back to her house, went in, and there was the coal merchant, sooty as ever and grinning from ear to ear as he handed me my pyjamas. What could I do but give him *cien pesetas*? He had won hands down all along the line. And all that talk about poverty! I had nothing but a thousand *peseta* note for which he gave me nine hundred *pesetas* change straight out of his bulging wallet. We shook hands and parted the best of friends.

On the fringe of the town there were several mountain streams with women washing clothes in them against the blue backcloth of the Sierra del Pozo. Women never seem to stop washing in Spain: morning, noon and night. I was fascinated watching two boys on a trotting donkey stallion having a wrestling match. They were sitting facing one another and each was trying to throw the other off. I never cease to admire the wonderful balance of these Andalusians. They are equally at home sitting forwards or backwards or sideways on a trotting or galloping animal and I believe that without any preliminary training they could ride a horse over the largest show jump.

By this time I had inevitably collected quite a following of children. Every foreigner must be prepared to play the rôle of the Pied Piper in Spain and the sooner you accept the rôle the better. Shrieking at the *niños* does not rid you of them, as I had learnt at Don Diego. As we got back to the *pueblo* I said I would buy them some sweets and they led me to a shop where I bought half a kilo. But as soon as I got out into the street and started to dole them out, three or four to each child, more and more children appeared from nowhere until I seemed to be surrounded by a thousand outstretched arms. In desperation I threw the remaining sweets into the air, causing a rugger scrum and much yelling from two poor little girls who got trodden underfoot. Realised I must try to think out a new technique of sweet distribution.

When I got back to the *posada* I went and wrote letters in the family sitting-room next to the kitchen. But one is never left undisturbed for long. Soon a mule dealer came in dressed in a grey cotton smock over corduroy trousers. He wanted to tell me how much he admired the Marquesa. He had seen her in the stable where he had just been to feed his nine mules. Next day he would take them home to Baza. Would I consider selling her? No, I explained, because she was not mine to sell. Would I ask her owner then? I was by now accustomed to offers for the Marquesa and had worked out a stock answer which, if not strictly speaking true, always deterred her admirers from bothering me further:

'She is the English Duke of Wellington and Ciudad Rodrigo's favourite mare,' I said. 'He always rides her when he comes to his estate.'

This middle-aged dealer, one of the handsomest men I ever saw, had such a gentle way of talking and such courtly manners that were he to discard his smock for a white tie and tails, he would hold his own at the grandest dinner-party.

I now heard ear-piercing screams coming from the covered yard. The pigs, to which the Marquesa had so much objected, were being weighed in scales suspended from the ceiling before being loaded into a lorry and driven away. I went to feed the old girl and found that all the sheep and pigs had left the stable. But the nine mules belonging to the aristocratic dealer were still there contentedly munching *paja y cebada*.

My friend the pig dealer had gone home having seen his purchases safely onto the lorry. The men at supper were chiefly connected with the dam and a fascinating young Sevillian electrician was the object of Maria's flashing eyes to-night. As a token of her affection she finally plunged under the cosy-table and burnt his legs with a hot cinder.

WEDNESDAY, NOVEMBER 15

In the morning I set off for Tiscar. It was warm and sunny and the unmetalled road led up into the sierras and I determined to enjoy my own company at whatever the cost. Hit upon a plan which I subsequently put into operation for the rest of my ride: if I wanted to overtake somebody on the way I would trot steadfastly by them chanting 'Vaya Usted con Dio-o-o-o-o.' If I had been dawdling along or sitting contemplating the scenery while the Marquesa had her lunch break and I heard hoofs approaching I would climb up into the saddle with the help of a bank or rock and go off at a good canter. I simply had to have the day to myself if I was to shine in the social life of the *posadas* at night. But on this ride I did not have to resort to either of the above stratagems. I was passed by two lorries in twelve kilometres but met nobody either walking or riding. The mountains were thickly planted with pines and I saw a large white notice board which read: *Ministerio de Agricultura. Patrimonio Forestal del Estado*.

Tiscar is a Grimm's fairy-tale village, an *aldea* as opposed to a *pueblo*, having only about two hundred inhabitants. It sprawls down a rocky gorge at the head of which colossal crags dwarf a minute Moorish castle and it is difficult to distinguish between the work of God and the work of man fashioned out of the same rock. We turned off the road down the steepest stone path I had negotiated since riding over the two Himalayan passes into Katmandu thirty years ago. Everywhere there were gushing, tumbling, sparkling mountain streams. Came to a mill with wheels underneath it lying parallel to the water instead of at right angles to it. Later learned that the flour ground in the mill is baked into bread on the premises in the only oven in the village. Just below it stood a row of three little crooked houses and outside the middle one two men were scalding the bristles off a vast slaughtered pig of the English large white breed, lying across a table. I asked for the *posada* and the elder of the men said: 'This is it.' He removed the saddle and led the Marquesa in through his very small front door (she could only just make it), past five women peeling a mountain of onions in the living-room, past the crooked stone stairs under which two little live pigs were sporting in a minute cellar —'These are for another year,' explained my landlord— along a rocky stone passage and into a dark stable where the family mule Española was munching *paja*. The litter was largely onion peelings. I asked for two kilos of barley which the Marquesa tucked her nose into. I was then taken upstairs and given the choice of four beds: two in a bed/store-room and two on a dark landing. I chose one of the latter as being the furthest from the little window, suffering as I was from a sore throat contracted by the abominable drains at Pozo Alcón.

Having unpacked my *alforjas* (nothing lost thanks to

69

the extra straps on the flaps) to the repeated cries of 'Water! Water!' from the bristle removers, I returned downstairs to find the whole of the pig's intestinal tube in a pale pink tangle on the table. The enchanting *posada* children offered to take me for a personally conducted tour of their village: there was Maria Bargar aged nine, and her brother Alberto, six, and their first cousins from over the way (whose father was working in Barcelona): Juanito aged twelve and little Vicente, bubbling over with charm, aged four.

They took me first to the great cave of the Virgin of Tiscar. Through the vast wall of rock above the village a powerful torrent has cut a deep ravine: below the road there is a waterfall and below this a huge natural cavern with a two-hundred-feet span. In a recess at the back, framed in stalagmites and stalactites, there is a tiny white statue of the Virgin, a copy of the famous one venerated in the church. You look across the ravine to the cave from a wooden platform guarded by a balustrade to prevent pilgrims from falling over into the water rushing and hissing below. This platform can only be reached by bending double and walking through a long low tunnel beside a little irrigation channel. It must require remarkable powers of organisation to deal with the crowds who come here from all the *pueblos* around, within a seventy-kilometre radius, for the *romería* on the feast of the Nativity of the Blessed Virgin on the 8th of September.

We next puffed and struggled up to the church which stands in a level courtyard above the road. It is pleasantly plain with dark brick walls and a roof of shallow cupolas. In the sanctuary there are some modern frescoes in the style of eleventh-century manuscript painting and at the back of the altar stands the famous image of the Virgin of Tiscar, patron of Quesada, a characteristic Spanish Madonna figure in the usual stiff brocade dress, very wide at the bottom. As a priest only comes out from Quesada to say Mass on Sundays, the Blessed Sacrament is not reserved at Tiscar. Adjoining the church is the sacristan's house and beyond it the huge pilgrim's hostel, where people sleep in rows on their straw palliasses at the time of the *romería*. On the other side of the courtyard there is the series of rocky crags at the head of the gorge, with the Moorish fortress perched almost imperceptibly among them, and there is a path cut in the rock, up which you can make the Stations of the Cross.

The children then led me down again to buy throat tablets at the village shop. The lady was astounded because I wanted the whole packet. She was accustomed to selling them in pairs. She shook them out of the packet onto the counter and proceeded to count them and to try to work out the total cost. In the end she had to call for the assistance of her husband to help her solve the problem.

We scrambled up and down the steep rock paths amid scenes of Arcadian beauty with the music of water forever in our ears: alongside every track ran a little rivulet tearing down to the torrent in the gorge below. There were wild fig trees growing out of crevices in the rock; vines trained over trellises to give shade outside the little houses, some of which were colour-washed Reckitt's blue; green strips of autumn-sown barley; almond and olive and peach trees and groves of poplars glittering with golden-brown leaves; a young man led a nice dapple-grey pony with pricked ears and an intelligent eye past us. All the young people wore gaily coloured clothes and the girls had red lipstick on their lips and undyed hair and looked so beautiful and so happy. And what washing! Jerseys and skirts and shirts and socks of vermilion and crimson lake and emerald and saffron and shocking pink drying on grey-green bushes and grey-blue rocks!

We scrambled down a precipitous path to the river where the ladies of the *posada* were on their knees washing the coral-coloured intestines in a misty blue pool. And by the time we had climbed home the intestines had beaten us to it and were now cosily coiled up in a large earthenware crock. Such a scene of domestic industry I have seldom witnessed: the eldest son of the house, Hilario, was turning chopped onions simmering in olive oil in a gigantic black frying-pan standing on an iron trivet over red embers: his lovely young wife, Felicidad (Happiness), far gone with child, was washing tripe in an enamel basin on the table with Juanito's mother helping her; his elder sister Paquita (engaged to an accordion player from Bellerda) and her mother Señora Bargar (my hostess) were crisping pimientos in smoking hot oil for a minute apiece so that they could afterwards be ground to powder; other women were cutting up onions, chopping parsley, peeling cloves of garlic and pounding peppercorns in a small brass mortar with a minute brass pestle. I was allowed to indulge in one of my favourite pastimes: blanching almonds.

At roughly 9 p.m. we all downed tools and sat round two tables put together and ate a simple form of *paella* directly out of another huge frying-pan with dessert spoons. It was sloppier than the Valencian variety but very good all the same: saffron-coloured rice with sliced potatoes, garlic and pimientos with the seeds left in so that you had to cram masses of bread into your mouth to prevent the roof being removed. '*Picante! Picante!*' observed Hilario shovelling it in.

Back to work after supper, for we were making *Morcillas Negras*—black puddings. Three large saucepans of rice were put on to boil in quick succession and as one lot of onions finished cooking it was tipped into the largest black *olla* (cauldron) I have ever seen while another lot replaced it in the frying-pan. The cooked rice joined the cooked onions in the *olla* together with a mountain of bread crumbs, several pints of rendered lard, the chopped parsley, pounded peppercorns, nutmeg and cinnamon with the following ingredients put through a large meat mincer: the crisped pimientos, about fifty cloves of garlic and at least two pounds of blanched almonds. Then the blood of the pig was poured in, the mixture stirred well together and fed into sections of the intestinal tube each tied at one end, the other end being pulled over a metal tube fixed to the mincer. When a section was full, it was removed and tied at the other end and there was a long sausage-shaped black pudding. This process took most of the night. The children and I retired to bed at 11.30 p.m. but all the women of the household and their neighbours worked through until 5 a.m. the next morning.

When I came down at eight o'clock to feed the Marquesa I counted eighty two loops of black pudding hanging from the beams. Breakfast was *sopa*, bread broken into a bowl with sugar and barley coffee poured over it. Got through as much as I could, leaving a few sops at the bottom. The poor women were yawning a lot but all up and about their business.

I took Juanito to school at Bellerda, the little village a mile further down the gorge. He got great prestige through riding the Marquesa. I rode in front for part of the way, when the path became so steep that I dismounted and led her. Bellerda was extremely pretty with a vine trained up the wall of nearly every house. The school was a long, low, new building standing in a small playground. The walls were of stone covered with smooth white-washed plaster and the windows were a sensible size to induce concentration, not great sheets of glass down to the ground. I left Juanito and the *aldea* behind me and rode on to explore the mountain mule-tracks. We got onto a very narrow one above a little river and I was wondering whether to proceed or turn back when a kind ploughman called after me saying that a horse could not get along that path. He then left his pair of sleek brown oxen and took the trouble to lead me back for a quarter

of a mile to a ford where we crossed the river and he put
me onto a safe path.

The track zig-zagged up and up while the river receded
into a narrow silver ribbon below. A precipice fell away
to my left and rose up to my right. I was far more
frightened than when being chased by the coal merchant.
It was impossible to turn round and I thanked God when
we eventually came to the stoniest little olive grove I have
ever seen. Got off and led the Marquesa back along the
way we came. I always get vertigo on narrow mountain
paths and do not like them.

When we got back to the *posada* in the late afternoon
everyone was busy in the kitchen making pork sausages
and white puddings. Three enormous bowls of mince
stood ready on the table, the one destined for the puddings
containing, among other delicacies, the colossal lights of
the pig, boiled and put through the mincing-machine and
the tripe treated in the same way.

That night we had a royal feast to celebrate the *matanza*
(pig killing): ten grown-ups sat round the two tables while
the four children sat on low chairs by the fire. We had
no plates or glasses or forks, just a spoon and a *navaja*
apiece.

First course: Pig's broth with bits of bread floating in it.
Second course: Extra good *cocido* (chickpea and potato soup
   with cloves of garlic).
Third course: Two large earthenware bowls containing
   slices of fried black pudding and assorted chitterlings
   eaten off the points of our *navajas* with pickled pimientos.
Fourth course: A delicious pork and chicken stew served
   in the *olla* in which it was cooked, swimming in yellow-
   ish brown gravy and accompanied by a mountain of
   olives. This was great fun: you jabbed your *navaja* into
   a bit of meat and took pot-luck; you gnawed all the

meat off the bone held in your fingers and tossed it over
your shoulder onto the floor. At one point Felicidad
fished out a hen's claw which she sucked clean with
great relish.

Fifth course: Pomegranates.

White wine was passed round and round in a *porrón*,
and after the excellent meal was over the women washed
the spoons and the serving dishes, scrubbed the tables
and swept up all the bones off the floor, leaving the
kitchen cleaner than many a one I have visited in the
British Isles, and what a way to solve the washing-up
problem!

Owing to bad weather and the extraordinary charm of
the children I stayed three nights at Tiscar feasting on
pork flesh. For lunch each day we had little titbits of
tenderloin and liver grilled in hot embers and eaten off
the points of our *navajas* with wonderful Spanish bread.
One morning I went and watched this being made in the
bakehouse attached to the tiny mill just above the *posada*.
A youth with a wooden-pronged pitch-fork was stuffing
the vast stone oven with brushwood which had been
brought there on the miller's mule. Then he set it alight
and it roared away for about a quarter of an hour, then
he raked the ash to one side and put in a hundred round
flat loaves which had been silently rising in rows on
wooden shelves and tables under linen cloths, then he
shut the iron door and left the loaves to bake into the
most delicious bread you could wish to eat.

On my last afternoon, while the rain poured down,
I retired to the bed/store-room beyond my landing to
try to catch up with my diary, writing on the end of a
treadle sewing-machine. There was a string stretched
across the two beds with dresses and coats on clothes-
hangers strung along it. There was a barrel of barley in
one corner and a good sample of a distorting mirror

covered with brown spots on one of the walls. On another there was an oleograph of the Blessed Virgin appearing to the souls in purgatory who seemed blissfully unaware of the flames licking their lower limbs, so intent were they on the heavenly vision above. 'Some shall be saved, yet so as by fire.'

When I went to the stable to feed the Marquesa little Vicente came too and proceeded to fling both his arms round the mule Española's hind legs. I remonstrated and pulled him hastily away but he struggled free and hugged her legs again exclaiming: '*Muy buena Española.*' And she certainly was very good for she never moved anything but her great ears which went forward in appreciation of the affection shown to her by the little boy.

Felicidad had begged me to come and see her house lower down the village before I went away, so hand in hand with Vicente we slithered together down the mud and rock path, approached the vine-covered porch, entered the front door and walked straight into the carcass of an enormous split pig! I was told the *matanza* had been at five o'clock this morning and all the poor women were hard at it again: black puddings, white puddings, sausages . . . onions, garlic, tripe, lights, herbs, spices, rice, almonds, breadcrumbs, and yards and yards of my old friends the pale pink intestines. Alberto had made a balloon of the pig's bladder stuck into a short piece of bamboo: the only toy I saw in Tiscar apart from skipping ropes.

Again fourteen of us sat down to supper which was on the table in a colossal frying-pan. Felicidad's mother, who lives with her, said grace including two Hail Mary's which we all joined in. She was an old lady of great dignity with a lined and leathery face and the calm beauty of suffering accepted. She told me later that she had had ten children and lost five and that the lovely Felicidad was her youngest.

Eating habits

We did not have a five-course feast as at the first *matanza*, but one great mess of pottage in the frying-pan containing chickpeas, onions, potatoes, pimientos, garlic, saffron, and lumps of streaky pork. In place of the usual fresh fruit we had home-bottled peaches from the Bargar's orchard. Hilario (Felicidad's husband) told me that they also have their own almond trees and olives and grow enough barley to feed Española and visiting beasts at the *posada*. He also discoursed on different eating customs (we had been given forks at this meal but nobody used them except myself and Felicidad who had received them as a wedding present). Some time ago, he said, he had gone to work in Madrid for a year and a friend of his who had been a waiter told him that at the hotels each person used several knives and forks and spoons and plates and glasses at every meal. Did I think this was really true? And what was the point of it? I admitted that it was, in fact, true, but that I could not see the point of it. The custom in Tiscar, I assured him, was far more sensible and friendly, as well as saving the women a lot of work.

At this *matanza* I had actually come in for the cooking of the black pudding. On the floor three purple serpents floated in a shallow crock of blood and water waiting their turn to be boiled. Beside them in a wide round basket further serpents reclined, draining on a cotton cloth, having been boiled. On a large iron trivet sat a great black *olla* with a host of wriggling serpents simmering in it. When they boiled too fast someone would throw a little cold water onto the pine-wood fire to damp it down. This is the way you control your cooking heat in Andalusia. The serpents were the black puddings, which the women had been making all day, enclosed in lengths of the pig's faithful intestinal tube. After supper they set to work again to finish off the white puddings and the sausages and to feed the mixtures into the remainder of the intestines via the mincer.

Entertaining Vicente

I sat in a corner by the fire and wrote a considerable part of my report on Ford's *Gatherings from Spain* for Jock Murray. The interruptions were many and varied but by this time I had become impervious to them: people kept standing between me and the only light, a circa 15-watt naked electric bulb hanging from the ceiling in the middle of the room. The older women kept commenting on how remarkable it was that I could write so fast when they could not write at all; then Vicente tried to deflate Alberto's pig's-bladder balloon and there was a lot of yelling. Eventually I stopped writing and took naughty little Vicente onto my knee and jogged him up and down playing *mulos*. Then I went through my limited art repertoire, drawing the usual *burros*, *caballos*, and *cocodrilos*, working up to my two masterpieces of St George and the Dragon and St James and the Moor. The little four-year-old *niño* then fell asleep in my arms, where he remained until Felicidad insisted on taking me up to her bedroom to show me her wedding presents.

All her girl friends came up too and I was shown embroidered sheets, nightdresses galore, pants and petticoats and finally the layette which provoked much giggling, especially when the mackintosh sheet was produced. Behind the double bed there was a glass-fronted niche containing a large plaster figure of the Holy Child in the crib with the young couple's wedding bouquet laid beside it and a coloured picture of St Damian, Apostle to the Lepers. Felicidad gave me a pamphlet about him and a copy of a Jesuit magazine she takes in. Most of her generation in the south of Spain can read and write, education having made much progress under the present regime: it is the grandmothers who are largely illiterate.

I had throughout my tour admired the local earthenware bowls out of which we ate, and the amphorae which are still used for carrying and storing water, there being a special wooden stand in every house into which they fit. When we returned to the kitchen Felicidad showed me with pride, some ugly modern plates arranged for show along the mantelpiece, and a green plastic cruet: further wedding gifts. Blast and damn all plastic consumer goods seeping in to spoil the virgin beauty of Tiscar.

SATURDAY, NOVEMBER 18

Early in the morning, when it was still dark, I had a call to the stables and in stumbling down to answer it I woke the two little pigs under the stairs who woke my landlord by their screams who thought it was a thief. 'It's only the English Señora!' I shouted nervously: whereupon he kindly switched on the light to reveal me crouching under Española, and discreetly returned to his bedroom on the ground floor.

When I came down dressed, at eight o'clock, the ceiling decoration excelled the most beautiful Adam plasterwork both in colour and design; for added to the purple loops of black puddings there were carmine loops of sausages and shell-pink loops of white pudding, all of them exuding a most delicate scent—which an Adam ceiling does not.

Maria and Juanito now accompanied me on a farewell visit to the vast and mysterious cave. I wish I could convey something of the simplicity of these Andalusian village children: they possess no toys bar those provided by a pig's inside; they eat the plainest of food and have no outings to the seaside in luxury motor-coaches; they have never been to a cinema nor watched television; they live in a non-atomic age knowing nothing of the world beyond the two *pueblos* on either side of them, Quesada and Pozo Alcón. And yet even the older ones appear to enjoy a sense of fun and wonder which it is increasingly difficult to find in a land of plenty where God is the Internal Combustion Engine and children's teeth are ruined at an

79

early age by surfeits of sweets. What is the answer? How can one preserve a balance between poverty and plenty so that true happiness is not corrupted by a false sense of values? Of course I do not know. If I did I should have solved the riddle of the Universe.

On our return to the *posada* I was given a small earthenware bowl containing the pig's brains grilled on pinewood embers. Eaten with bread and salt it was a breakfast to remember.

Sorrowfully, tearfully, I gave Española a farewell pat, then kissed and hugged each of the children in turn, thanked my host and hostess for their marvellous hospitality, and reluctantly rode away.

Tiscar is far more impressive from the Quesada side than from that of Pozo Alcón and I kept having to stop to take photographs of the great rock screen and the tiny Moorish tower and the grey mountains which appeared through the cutting and which seemed to be floating towards the infernal regions on a sea of white cloud. About five kilometres beyond the village I noticed a boy with two donkeys turning off along a track to the left. I followed and passed them as it was obviously a short cut to Quesada. It rejoined the road some way further on and then another track branched off, so that three parts of the journey can be made by mule-tracks.

When I got to Quesada I had half a mind to proceed to Cazorla. Then I thought the Marquesa would like a feed so I led her down a very steep cobbled lane to the main street which was narrow but tarred. There was a nice *posada* with a bedroom which had two panes of glass in the window and two panes broken out. The stable was stuffy and smelly with all the household refuse thrown down on the litter, not at all up to the usual standard of compost. The poor Marquesa was tied up close to a huge pile of logs and they kept slipping down between her legs (later, when some mules left I moved her lower down).

A poet

I bought two kilos of barley in the shop next door as the
landlord had not got any, then went and called on the
párroco.

Don Antonio, an exceptionally charming man, was
sitting at a desk in his office, wreathed in smiles and busy
receiving an endless stream of parishioners who came to
him for papers to be signed and questions to be answered.
I asked him to tell me the story of the Virgin of Tiscar.
He welcomed me most warmly to his *pueblo*, invited me
to luncheon, promised to tell me the story afterwards and
in the meantime insisted on taking me to the town hall
to meet the *Alcalde* (mayor), Don Antonio Navarrete,
who is a nature poet of distinction and has recently published a collection of lyrics describing the rocks and
streams and birds and plants of his wild sierras. I subsequently showed this book to the American poet Gamel
Woolsey, the wife of Gerald Brenan, and here is her translation of one of the *Alcalde de Quesada's* poems. . . .

THE JACKDAWS

There are mountains like brooding hens to hatch jackdaws
With their croaking and their mineral feathers:
So that the unmoving cry of the darkness
May knife-pierce the eyelids of the dawn.

They are children of stone, like water and lichen,
And carry through the wind ancient messages
Of nights without horse-breaking and without cooing.

They ignore the birds, because their pure sheen
Limits them to a flight of broken crystals,
In the folds of hidden geology;
And they stare at the flesh which flies, daughter of other
  flesh,
Gazing at it with a gaze of quartz.

A painter

When a jackdaw dies an ivy plant appears
In the crevice where it had its nest:
It is so that the stones renew themselves
Instead of with children of their entrails.

I was now led by the priest and the poet across the plaza to a pleasant little picture gallery, just completed and containing the works of Rafael Zabaleta, son of a Quesada cloth merchant who died last year at the early age of fifty-two. Thanks to his friend the cultivated *Alcalde*, this painter had been honoured in his own country. His early work shows the influence of blue Picasso, then there are traces of pointillism, Braque, Matisse, the Douanier. A master of composition he comes into his own painting his *pueblo* and its surrounding sierras and some of his harvest scenes are worth a special journey to Quesada to see. I was deeply moved to find this nest of culture in such a remote mountain fastness: the theologian, the painter and the poet.

I returned to the *posada* to change into a jersey and skirt. My landlady was suitably impressed when I said I was going to lunch with the parish priest. I told her that I had now definitely decided to stay the night as it was unlikely that the meal would be over before 4 p.m., there were two churches to see and it got dark soon after six.

Back in the presbytery Don Antonio introduced me to his sweet old mother and father who lived with him, and his mother told me she had two younger sons both studying for the priesthood in the Diocesan seminary at Jaén. The house is one in a row, the small rooms having tiled floors and the study containing glass-fronted bookcases crammed with theological works in Latin and Spanish, including complete editions of St Teresa and St John of the Cross.

For luncheon we had rabbit and potato stew followed

by liver, and ending with a surprisingly English beige
cornflour pudding sprinkled with sugar and cinnamon.
When we had finished the priest told me, with much
patience and repetition, speaking very slowly and clearly
so that I could understand him, the story of the Virgin
of Tiscar. . . .

'St Isicio, disciple of St Peter, was Bishop of Carcesi,
Cazorla and Quesada, in the first century. It was he who,
according to tradition and the history of Escudero de la
Torre, brought the image of the Virgin of Tiscar which
was venerated by the people until the Moorish invasion
in the eighth century.

'When the Moors conquered Tiscar, they took the
image of the Blessed Virgin prisoner for six hundred and
three years. They did not destroy it but used it as a hostage
with which to extort payments from their Christian
subjects.

'In 1309 the Archbishop of Toledo Don Gutierrez
Gomea and the Infante Don Pedro of Castile, conquered
Quesada and ten years later Tiscar. As they were march-
ing on the latter the Muslim governor of the fortress,
Mahommed Handoun, thinking that the motive for the
attack was to recover the image of the Virgin, hurled this
into the torrent below the great cave known as "The Cave
of the Water". But instead of being broken into a thousand pieces by the force of the stream against the rocks, it
floated safe and sound to the bank. Twice more the in-
furiated Moor hurled it back into midstream and twice
more it returned to him undamaged. The fourth time he
pushed it back into the raging torrent he struck at the
head of the image with his sword and slashed the Virgin's
forehead after which she finally sank. This was told to the
Infante and the Archbishop after they had taken possession
of Tiscar by one of their Muslim captives. They at once
hurried to the great cave, whereupon the sacred image
immediately reappeared so that they were able to lift it

safely onto the bank. It was subsequently repaired and put in order by a Christian craftsman but he was unable to efface the scar on the Virgin's forehead made by the infidel's sword.

'Tiscar became Christian once again and the miraculous image was placed in the church built on the site of the Muslim prison where Our Lady had spent so many centuries as a hostage of the Moors.

'Some years later the Archbishop decided to move the precious image to Toledo and with this object in view he had it tied onto a horse. He rode behind on another horse but when the Virgin reached the second watch-tower on the road to Quesada, the image slipped off its horse and returned miraculously to Tiscar. The Archbishop and his train turned their horses round and hurried back to the wild and rocky stronghold where they found the image back in its place in the church. The Archbishop then perfectly understood that the Blessed Virgin wished to remain in the prison where she had spent six hundred years. So the image remained in the church until 1936 when the reds hammered it to pieces and threw them into the torrent below the cave.

'In 1939 the sculptor Hinqueras made an image of the Virgin of Tiscar which he was able to copy faithfully from photographs. Three years later the scar appeared on the Virgin's forehead which she had received from the angry Moorish governor in 1319. It may be seen to this day.'

The story finished, we talked about the Anglican Church and the doctrine of *infalibilidad*. Theology is the only subject on which I can have anything approaching an intellectual conversation in Spanish because the terms are the same as in English, both being of Latin origin: you simply substitute *ad* for *ty* and it nearly always works: *Trinidad, Caridad, infalibilidad*; or *ción* for *tion*: *concepción, contrición, transubstanciación*, and that works equally well.

A tour of Quesada

Don Antonio was astounded when I told him that
several religious orders in the Church of England recited
the whole of the Divine Office in Latin, and how widely
read were the Spanish mystics by Anglicans, both lay and
religious. Before taking me off to see his churches he
presented me with a book on the Rosary. My tour was
now becoming like George Borrow's the other way round:
whereas he distributed sacred literature I was receiving
so much that I should soon have to hire a donkey to
carry it.

We went first to the smaller of the two Quesada
churches, pleasant provincial baroque dated 1634. Then
we walked uphill, through streets with more pots of
flowers to the balcony than in any other *pueblo* I have seen,
to the parish church above the town, built on the site of
the Moorish castle of which it retains the tower. The
interior is cluttered up with images of little merit but
Don Antonio told me he was going to transform it and
clear a lot of stuff out. He also said that the Virgin of
Tiscar is carried here each May, fourteen kilometres along
the mountain road on the shoulders of his male parishioners, including those of the literary *Alcalde*, and returns
to her own village at the end of August in time for her
birthday on September 8 when the great pilgrimage takes
place. He then went on to say that the British had said
some unkind things about Spain: that we did not understand that Franco's rule was quite different from that of
Mussolini or Hitler; that before the civil war communist
infiltration was rife; that Franco had saved the country
and preserved the Catholic Faith; that there was great
respect for the priesthood in these parts (indeed I had
seen two men come up and kiss his hand in the street),
and that the people were poor but happy, and that everyone had enough to eat.

As I was producing and rearing my son during the
civil war, 1936-9, my ignorance of its origins is profound

I get weighed on the pig scales

(when I have finished my homework on *Don Quixote*, I hope to do some on Gerald Brenan's *Spanish Labyrinth* and Thomas Hughes' *Spanish Civil War*) so that I can only judge a small corner of Spain as I see it to-day. Having spent six months in fascist Italy in 1928 and been present at the famous *adunata* in Rome on the eve of the Abyssinian war in 1935 and having lived in Berlin for three months in 1933, I can only agree with Don Antonio that the present regime in Spain has created a very different atmosphere to that in the hundred per cent fascist countries of Italy and Germany before World War II. Naturally there is known to be a certain amount of anti-clericalism among people whose husbands or fathers were shot by the nationalists and who would rather die than darken the doors of the church: but I didn't myself come across any of these, whereas in Italy every other man I sit next to in a train or a country 'bus hates the church and there is an aggressively anti-clerical atmosphere up and down the country which is very unpleasant.

After Saturday evening devotions in the little baroque church, where the Hail Mary's were said nice and slowly so that I was not left miles behind, I returned to my *posada* to be greeted by the now familiar screams of pigs being weighed in the narthex. A bright idea struck me: I would get weighed myself together with my equipment to see just how much weight the Marquesa had to carry up and down the sierras. So I queued up and took my turn sitting in the rope scales, followed by my saddle with its great iron stirrups, then by my *alforjas*, boots, and vast oilskin coat. Total weight: 131 kilos or rather over 18 stone! The saddle alone weighed just on half a hundred-weight. Decided to augment the Marquesa's already generous corn ration to that of a heavyweight hunter in full work—16 lb. per day.

For supper I had two fried eggs and dry bread, followed by grapes. I was not very hungry, having had a three-

86

course lunch at the presbytery. Afterwards I sat round an open brazier in the cobbled narthex and talked to a man of unknown profession who was anxious that I should warm myself. He offered me some of his supper of dry bread and raw fish but I protested that I was full right up. The other guests consisted of a young married couple who went out and bought their supper and came back and ate it at the brazier: bread and herrings. My landlord (whose right arm was shrivelled below the elbow—he told me he was born like it) and his wife had fried fresh sardines which they ate with their fingers, using their *navajas* with which to cut off huge hunks of bread. Loaves and fishes everywhere: the symbols of Christ and the Eucharist.

I filled my hot-water bottle with an enamel mug from water heated in a frying-pan—a very skilled job—gargled in strong vinegar provided by my landlady, and went to sleep sucking penicillin throat tablets which tasted of peppermint.

SUNDAY, NOVEMBER 19

The next morning I woke up at 6.30 a.m. so got up to go to the early Mass in the Parish Church. But when I got downstairs the great double doors of the *posada* were locked and bolted and barred as effectively as in any convent. I fumbled for a light switch and eventually found it behind a huge square pillar. The feeble light revealed two men sleeping on palliasses so soundly that I had not the heart to wake them up and ask for assistance. The church bells were ringing and it was most frustrating being quite unable to move the bolts or turn the key. So I went and got the bucket of barley from under my bed and fed the Marquesa who was enchanted to see me so early.

The 9.30 Mass was very full, including a good proportion of men, and most people received Holy Communion.

In spite of the fact that Don Antonio had spent a lot of the previous day entertaining me, leaving little time for the preparation of his sermon, he preached an excellent one on the Gospel for the day, the Parable of the Grain of Mustard Seed and the Leaven.

After breakfast my landlord's sixteen-year-old son took me up into the loft to see his tame pigeons, about a dozen of them. They were very well housed with plenty of room and plenty of clean water, a bowl full of maize and an opening in the roof where they flew in and out as they pleased. Two of the hen birds were each sitting on two of their own eggs plus two small chicken eggs.

I called on Don Pedro, the tall young curate who had married Felicidad and Hilario at Tiscar. He lived with two of his sisters near the Parish Church in a little house which was in the process of being renovated. On the top floor there was a furnished sitting-room with a cosy-table, some chairs and two rocking-chairs. Eight girls were standing round the table having a lesson in the singing of the *Missa de Angelis*. There seems to be a strong movement in these parts to get the people to join in the Mass.

I went and said goodbye to Don Antonio and his parents and gave him a parting gift of a small picture of Blessed Edmund Campion out of my Missal. He talked delightedly of how many people had received Holy Communion at all three Masses this morning. Upon being questioned he said that there was a very rough track—'*un camin muy malo*'—from his *pueblo* to Cazorla ten kilometres away and he advised me to go by the road. Little did he know the effect which those magic words always had upon me: *un camin muy malo*. Nor of the passionate desire for adventure and beauty and solitude which they stirred up in my bosom.

I left Quesada after an early luncheon accompanied by my landlord's charming son: oh what marvellous manners all these Spanish teenage boys have! He walked down to the bottom of the town with me and put me on to the rocky and romantic *camin muy malo*. There were marvellous views looking back at the *pueblo* from this track with the big parish church standing right out against the skyline on the site of the fortress it has replaced.

About two kilometres out from Quesada we came to a little whitewashed chapel with a belfry. There was a hole in the locked door through which I could see the interior, derelict but for a statue of St Sebastian on the altar. As there was a nice wide patch of juicy grass, emerald green from the recent rains, in front of the chapel, I took off the Marquesa's bridle and let her graze while I sat on my large yellow sou'wester and read Ford. Then a dear old boy arrived on the scene with a Friesian cow on a long string. I said 'Good afternoon. I am English, I am on a tour in these mountains. I have come from . . .' He did not seem at all surprised but was preoccupied about something. I continued to read my book. At the end of ten minutes he came up and politely handed me a typewritten paper which said that the Mayor of Quesada granted him the sole grazing rights round the oratory of St Sebastian. I apologised profusely and offered him a five-peseta piece for usurping the grass which belonged exclusively to his cow. This he absolutely refused to take. So the Marquesa and I proceeded along our rough and lovely way to Cazorla.

Eventually we came to the upper of the two fortresses above the town, brilliantly illuminated by a stormy sunset. The *camin* was by now so *malo* and so steep that I dismounted and led the Marquesa down through the rocks and the slippery mud into the upper end of Cazorla with the second and far larger fortress standing on a hill in the midst of it. Then I remounted and rode past the ruined renaissance church of Santa Maria (gutted by the French in the Napoleonic wars) into a beautiful wide plaza. Here some children attached themselves to me and took me to the *posada*. The entrance was on an awkward corner half-way down a steep hill and as the Marquesa turned into the cobbled narthex her feet shot from under her and she came right down. As it takes me ten minutes to get out of an Andalusian saddle she was up again before I could dismount, whereupon she went straight down again a second time. I tried to get my leg quickly over the high cantle but without success: the poor old girl struggled up again complete with her load of eighteen stone. When I at last managed to get off, I led her into the large and airy stables at the back with three roomy compartments and plenty of litter. Thank goodness she had not cut herself in her falls but her shoes had worn very smooth and I decided to get a new set put on.

The bedroom wing of this *posada*, which is called the *Parador de la Estrela*, was rebuilt last year to attract the French tourists who flock here every summer (though how they have the nerve after what their great-grandfathers did to the best church, I don't know). My bedroom had a tiled floor, a window with glass in it, a basin with a cold tap and a non-distorting mirror above it. It was like coming to the Ritz after what I had been used to. There was one chair, but curiously enough nowhere at all to put my clothes, not even the customary pegs. I asked for a table and got a po cupboard but one cannot have everything even at the Ritz. It was at this *posada* that I first hit upon the brilliant idea of putting two thicknesses of brown paper down on the floor for a bedside mat. For the remainder of my tour this added greatly to my comfort.

Another Ritzy feature of this inn was a bathroom on the second floor with a W.C. which really worked and did not stink. Fortunately cold water only came out of both the hot and cold bath taps so that I was not tempted to have a bath. I did not want to wash the natural oil out of my skin, on the same principle that one must never groom a horse at grass. I would be certain to die of pneumonia in the next draughty *posada* I lodged in.

Before supper I went out and bought some more throat tablets and a large bottle of bronchial cough cure. I was now spitting like the natives though not in my bedroom nor in church. Had a delicious rice mess in the cold dining-room at 10 p.m. with baby globe artichokes in it and French beans and lumps of fat pork. My landlady was something of a cook.

MONDAY, NOVEMBER 20

Mass at 9 a.m. No dialogue. Breakfast consisted of a large glass of real coffee and a large *torta*, a sort of bun with sugar sprinkled over the top. A real treat. Thought I would try to look as chic as possible when I went out shopping (Cazorla being a big *pueblo* of 12,000 inhabitants), so I wore the smarter of my two jerseys with my Terylene skirt and black stockings. Soon realised that I was the subject of ridicule because of the latter: only old women wear them in these parts. I went and bought some nylons, then walked down to the barracks of the *Guardia Civil* to collect my mail which Rosemary Tonsen-Rye had angelically promised to deliver. Returned to *posada* and read all my letters in the family sitting-room, including four from my husband in Australia. A lot about centipedes in which he is passionately interested. I hoped he wouldn't bring any home.

When I went to give the Marquesa her augmented mid-day feed I counted fifteen mules, ponies and donkeys in the stables. Their owners leave them there when they come in to shop, the charge being two *pesetas* a time, which includes *paja* but not *cebada*. Talked to an old man and his wife in the narthex who had had a two-hour ride from their farm. They came in once a week to buy stores: a four-hour journey there and back.

Friendly pigs

As soon as the Marquesa had finished eating I attacked her with the dandy and brushed all the mud off her hocks and legs which she had collected yesterday along the *camin muy malo*. While I was bending low over my work two huge pigs (large whites) walked in from another section of the rambling stables and started to nose my hair. They did not know it, but early in December they too were for *la matanza*. I handed them some soggy Marie biscuits from the rucksack. They nosed me so lovingly, so trustingly, and soon their great intestines would be lying in heaps in the kitchen waiting to be filled with pudding mixture and to be hung in hundreds of loops from the beams of my landlord's shop.

My landlord, Francisco Diez, was a man of property. He owns this big *parador* which provides a good income from tourists in the summer and from stabled animals all the year round. Last year he bought two olive groves on the outskirts of the town, so he produces his own oil. His shop adjoining the narthex was a general store selling groceries, boots, shoes, socks, shirts, barley and all kinds of ironmongery.

Felipe was the odd job man at the *Parador de la Estrela*. He was small and wiry and wore a beret perpetually. He slept on a camp-bed just inside the great double doors of the narthex, for among many other things he was the doorkeeper in the house of his lord, Francisco Diez. But Felipe loved horses better than anything else, as his name implied, and was potty about the Marquesa: *'Sta muy docil! muy gorda!'* (she is very quiet, very fat) he kept exclaiming admiringly. And he took my tack to pieces and cleaned it very efficiently with lard.

Luncheon at 4 p.m. consisted of an oddly assorted mixed grill with little bits of tough steak, lumps of pork fat, three fried fresh sardines, a grilled thrush and some chips, all on the same plate. I hate eating small songbirds but did not like to offend my charming landlady who took real trouble over my meals, so I ate the bosom and gave the legs to the cats.

I exercised the Marquesa for about an hour in the evening, exploring a mountain path leading to the upper fortress. On the return ride I noticed that the makeshift wooden door on the south side of the ruined church of Santa Maria was open, so I dismounted on the off side onto a convenient step, leaving the mare loose. Only the four walls remain of what must have been a fine late renaissance church. The floor was grass-grown, with washing spread out on it. When I went back to the Marquesa she was *still standing exactly as I had left her:* the perfect sightseer's hack. So I mounted from the step on the off side and rode home.

I answered letters in the family sitting-room while Manuelo, my landlord's eldest son aged seventeen, sat opposite studying electronics. Felipe came in to ask if he might give the Marquesa her evening feed. We all three got talking and I tried to explain to him that his name meant 'lover of horses', and that my father and my nephew, both cavalrymen and great lovers of horses, were called by it too. I said hippos means a horse, that hippopotamus means a river horse and philhippos a lover of horses. He failed to understand why I was comparing him to a hippopotamus but smiled appreciatively all the same.

Felipe then told me that he used to work on the precipitous sierras behind the *pueblo* on the electric light scheme. He had a real appreciation of the beauties of his province and kept saying how *bonito* was the countryside surrounding Cazorla. He told me he had often walked to the source of the Guadalquivir, four hours there and four hours back. I wished he could guide me there but feared he was too busy. Señor Diez, having had two operations for duodenal ulcers and having the shop to mind plus all his other business, badly needed all the help he could get. There was another old boy, bent and emaciated, who helped around the place and a sweet old daily woman who talked such broad Andaluz that I could hardly understand a word she said.

TUESDAY, NOVEMBER 21

My sore throat was still very bad at night but it was such a sunny morning that I decided I would ride up into the mountains to try to find the source of the Guadalquiver on my own and to blow the cold out of my head. There is a motor road which goes to it by a long and roundabout route but this I despised. So I rode out past the ruined church and along a stream and asked the way at a farm. The man told me in some detail but as I proceeded the path became very steep and divided and subdivided until eventually, to my great delight, it joined a fairly wide, smooth and well-defined *patrimonio forestal* track in a government afforestation area. Rode up this to the right, fondly imagining that it would eventually lead over a pass in the great black wall of rock above us. Then a cloud descended so that I could only see about fifty yards ahead in the mist, and it started to rain. Put on my yellow sou'wester and the hooded oilskin which covered me completely as well as the Marquesa's quarters down to her hocks. The track was still clear but conditions were definitely unpleasant: should we turn round and go back the way we came? No, this was not the way the British Empire was won, so lured by that mysterious impulse which draws you to the top of a mountain, I rode up into the cloud, rattling round the rosary in the rain.

Never before have I realised how friendly, how almost human, trees can be in high sierras. Never again shall I say anything nasty about conifers. I have no head for heights, so whenever the path led over bare rock, with God knows what dreadful precipice falling away into the

mist, I was petrified. But when it led back among the pine
trees I felt perfectly safe. They seemed to receive me with
open arms and to say: 'Come into us. We will protect you
from the abyss; we will keep you safe.' Then triumph!
We had apparently reached the top of the pass! And on
the far side the track descended steeply and suddenly out
of the cloud and a great new landscape was spread out
before us: rocky crags, stone pines, rolling green hills,
and below them the interminable olive groves of this
province of Jaén with a distant *pueblo* miles away to the
left looking like an overturned waste-paper basket. There
was no sign of the source of the river but round a hairpin
bend appeared a large square golden tower sitting on
top of a rounded grass-covered hill. We descended in
further hairpins past little mountain farms and at the end
of an hour another *pueblo* came into view with a Moorish
castle in front of it and rows of new housing estates on
the far side. Should I have lunch there and ride back to
Cazorla afterwards? Or should I, in spite of being without
luggage, stay the night and send a wire to the *Parador de
la Estrela* saying I was safe and would return to-morrow?
A kilometre outside the *pueblo* I asked a muleteer what its
name was: 'Cazorla,' he said.

Damn the source of the Guadalquivir. It can keep itself to itself. Pride goes before a fall. I have never stopped
patting myself on the back about my brilliance at cross-
country navigation; my wonderful bump of locality
acquired through forty years in the hunting field. And
now in a common mountain mist I had lost my bearings
completely.

That evening I decided to go to a doctor about my
throat. I was directed to one by the barman in the excellent café in the main plaza where I often went to drink
coffee or chocolate. The medico turned out to be the
leading gynaecologist of Cazorla. However he most kindly
examined my throat in his very up-to-date surgery and

prodded my face and said I had pus in my sinuses which was going down into my throat and causing the trouble. He prescribed a gargle, inhalant, tablets and a course of four penicillin injections. He then went next door to his office and typed precise directions on the back of the prescriptions so that I should understand the treatment perfectly. I asked him his fee but he refused to take a single *peseta* saying I was a guest in his country.

I went back to the plaza where I found a chemist and asked him to make up the prescriptions. While he was doing so I indulged myself with a lovely cup of hot chocolate in my favourite café. Then returned for the drugs which cost 231 *pesetas* (about 27/-). By a great bit of luck there was a *praticante* (district male nurse) in the back of the shop so I was able to have my first intra-muscular injection on the spot. I made a great fuss and he said '*Quieta!*' to me like the muleteers say to their mules. I must say I have never had such a quick and painless injection in my life and when I congratulated the *praticante* on his skill he smiled and said, '*Profesional!*'

Having quickly become part of the Diez family in the way one does in Spain, I now had my meals with them at their cosy-table instead of in the cold *comedor*. Before supper I helped Manuelo with his English which he had been learning at school for the past two years. He had a translation book called the *Segundo Curso de Inglés*, out of which he was studying the following passage:

'THE ENGLISH AT WORK
'*Ploughing*. Look at this photograph [a very bad one indeed]. Perhaps you are surprised to see a girl, she is English [and wearing a felt hat], driving a heavy tractor? This is because during the last war, when most Englishmen were fighting in the Army or working in factories, there were not enough people to work on the land. And in wartime every piece of land must be

cultivated to produce food which cannot come from other countries. This girl is a member of the Women's Land Army. She is preparing the soil with a tractor plough to receive the seed which will be planted later.'

After supper Señora Diez and I went and sat round the bonfire on the cobbles of the narthex under the most enormous chimney hood I have ever seen. I paced it and it measured roughly 15 by 18 feet and you could look straight up the short chimney at the starry sky. Sent Felipe off to get a bottle of wine for himself and the two mule-teers who made up the rest of the company, while my landlady revealed to my horror that the whole of the ground floor was to be rebuilt in the spring which would entail the destruction of this titanic fireplace. I tried to explain that it is against all the interests of her trade to do this: that it is a unique feature and a great part of the charm of her *Parador*. She admitted that all the French tourists photographed the fireplace but said that she must have a nice kitchen. The present one is literally out of doors in an open yard to the side of the inn with a large black hood protecting the charcoal stoves but otherwise completely exposed to the elements.

'Of course you must have a good kitchen indoors,' I said, 'but there is plenty of room to build one without destroying this beautiful and extremely practical feature of the place!' She smiled sweetly but did not give an inch.

So 'Progress' has come to Cazorla. I would like to start a society for the protection of *posadas*, to preserve the many architectural curiosities which they contain for future generations of travellers.

While the men drank *vino tinto* and told me the way I ought to have gone to reach the source of the Guadal-quiver, I sat sadly over the bonfire on which water was heating in a little *olla* for my hot-water bottle. Then I filled it with an enamel soup ladle. I love the *cosas de*

España and cannot bear to think of them changing. I don't want to be able to fill my bottle from an electric kettle; and being an animist I wanted to cry because this large black chimney, like the large white pigs, was awaiting its *matanza*.

WEDNESDAY, NOVEMBER 22

Had the most Ritzy morning of my tour. I felt wonderful after a night of healing sleep and the drugs had done their stuff. At eleven o'clock Señora Diez brought me my breakfast in bed: a glass of *café-au-lait* and six Marie biscuits. In spite of her predilection for tearing down buildings, she was infinitely kind to human beings. Dozed and read until 1 p.m., when I got up and went to my café to read *Don Quixote* and drink chocolate.

After luncheon Felipe and I took the Marquesa to the forge. Having accompanied Pitirri with two horses to the blacksmith on my first tour I knew the ropes and shirked the donkey work. The smith measured the old girl's feet and found a ready made set of shoes which fitted them very nicely. Horse shoes in Spain are broader and flatter than in England. Felipe held up one foot after the other while the smith rasped the hooves and nailed the shoes on, hammering two distinct notes on his anvil like the *Niebelungen*. You may laugh at the Spanish system but it results in a smith being able to shoe a horse in half the normal time: thirty-five minutes by my watch. It cost seventy-five *pesetas*, about 9s. 6d.

On the way home Felipe raved again about the Marquesa's temperament. '*Muy docil! Muy docil!*' he kept repeating. He had never known a horse to be so quiet at the forge and he pulled back the hair from his forehead revealing a deep and ugly scar which he had got while holding up a horse's hind foot some years ago.

Felipe lifted on the half-hundredweight saddle for me

98

and I rode the exemplary Marquesa up towards the top fort as we both needed the exercise. But at the end of an hour it rained so hard that we had to hurry back, both enveloped in our communal oilskin. It was very annoying as I longed to explore the Sierra de Cazorla for at least a week, pottering from one mountain *pueblo* to another and riding round the great lake, the Pantano del Tranco de Beás. But as the weather had now broken good and proper I would have to alter my plans.

That evening I went to the house of the charming *praticante* to have my second injection. He picked up my copy of *Don Quixote* and said he had read it five times but preferred Homer to Cervantes. Delighted to find that he was also a *punaise de Sacristie* like myself, as we both met there after devotions when I went to enquire about the catechism campaign which the parish priest had preached about.

THURSDAY, NOVEMBER 23

I went to Mass at 8.30 a.m.—St Clement Pope and Martyr—and noticed in my Missal that next day was the Feast of St John of the Cross. As I had learned from Annie's *Guide Bleu* that he died in Ubeda in 1591 I decided that whatever happened I must ride there. Perhaps the rain was providential after all?

I told everyone at the *posada* of my intention when I got home and asked the Señora to hard boil two eggs for my lunch. Don Quixote and Richard Ford were always complaining about rascally inn-keepers and the shameless way in which they overcharged. On the contrary I have everywhere found my bills extremely reasonable and fair. My account at the Ritz, Cazorla (*Parador de la Estrela*), for four nights and three full days was five hundred *pesetas* (just under £3) and included my being made to feel a member of the family; glass in my bedroom window; a very comfortable bed; two full meals a day and real coffee for breakfast; stabling, *cebada y paja* and the attentions of Felipe for the mare.

Felipe called a mule-track a *carril* instead of a *camino*. He walked beside us out of the town and tried to explain where we could get on to one but I missed it. Proceeded for just on two hours along the road which first descended on to, and then crossed, the plain to Peal de Becerro. There are some ancient tombs there but on enquiry I learned that they were five kilometres from the *pueblo* in another direction to that of Ubeda so I had to choose between them and San Juan. A little further on I made the most fatal mistake of my tour: *I did not believe the directions of a muleteer*. The distance between Cazorla and Ubeda is actually forty-eight kilometres by road, but owing to my bungling we certainly covered far more.

The muleteer told me that if I continued down the road I would come to a bridge across the Guadalquivir and should then turn immediately to the left along a lane leading to the *Cortijo Puente de Roma*. But I thought I knew better. I was fed up with the metalled road which had been tarred since the publication of my map on which it was marked in white, so that I mistook it for another. Away to the north I saw a track after my own heart and against my better judgement I let myself be lured towards it, riding boldly across country through deep plough. We had to jump up a stone-faced bank from a ploughed field into an olive grove and eventually we reached the lovely wide muddy lane and trotted and cantered happily along it. When we came to a nice grassy bank by a stream I removed the Marquesa's bridle and the *alforjas* and turned her loose to graze while I ate my eggs and bread and cheese and chocolate and an apple. A man rode by on a mare and to my great surprise the Marquesa actually stopped eating to follow them. The man caught hold of her halter rope and I ran up and led her back to her lunch.

This proved to be the only time on the whole of our four weeks' tour that the Marquesa walked off.

Two boys now galloped past us going flat out along the track on two thirteen-hand ponies, both riding in halters and without stirrups. They raced on for a few hundred yards and then turned along a path to the right leading to a farmhouse. It is wonderful to go thus backwards in time to the life of a hundred years ago when both one's transport and one's fun depends on the horse and not on the internal combustion engine.

Rode on after lunch for a further three kilometres but began to feel uneasy about the north-easterly direction in which the track was going, so I rode up to the next farmhouse and was told that I was on the road to Santo Tomé. I now had to cut back across country in an attempt to find the bridge over the beastly and ever elusive Guadalquivir.

We proceeded along muddy tracks which rode nearly as deep as the Old Berks country. The poor Marquesa was having a tough day. I looked nostalgically over rolling downs of ploughland to the blue Sierra de Cazorla. The clouds had lifted and I could see the upper fortress sitting sunning itself on its round green hill. We rode through a neat new settlement for farm workers and asked the way again; I was directed along a lane past some huge thatched shelters under which long orange tobacco leaves were drying; then at last we came to the bridge over the famous river which was yellow and muddy. I felt very annoyed with it for leading me a dance on two occasions.

'You can't hold a candle to our own rivers,' I told it. 'They are clear and you are cloudy; they have sinuous weeds flowing rhythmically with the stream and you have none; they have grassy banks with figwort and willow herb and purple loosestrife and evergreen alkanet growing along them: your banks are dry and dreary mud. In fact you have nothing to recommend you and I am not going to bother about you any more. Only your name is romantic.'

But the river sprites pursued us and led us up the metalled main road. Had I followed my instinct and turned left along a sandy lane close to the bridge we would have got to the Cortijo Puente de Roma and eventually to Ubeda entirely by untarred side roads. But I had got so confused in my map-reading, owing to the evil influence of the Guadalquivir, that I did not realise until it was too late that this was the lane described by the muleteer outside Peal. Sometimes we found well-worn paths through the olive groves which cut off great loops of the road. Then the latter straightened out and there was nothing for it but to ride along the untarred verge. After we had jogged about six kilometres away from the river a workman caught up with us on his bicycle. A bicyclist is the one type of traveller you cannot beat in the road game because if he really wants to talk he will pedal hard uphill to keep pace with your trot, and dismount and walk beside you going downhill. My companion said we still had seven kilometres to go to his *pueblo* of Torreperogil and that it was nine kilometres on to Ubeda from there which meant that we would not reach it till after dark. Made my usual agricultural conversation: there were no olive trees in England because it was too cold and damp. Then what did we do for oil? We imported it from Spain and Italy which made it very expensive so we did not use it very much, we ate butter instead. How dreadful! Fancy having to eat butter instead of oil. I remarked how surprised I was to see so many pigs of the English breed in Andalusia, *cerdos grandes blancos* I called them. Yes they got bigger and produced more fat than the native breed he explained. Spaniards have not got the present English craze for lean bacon, pork fat being highly prized. Your native pigs have orange bristles, I wanted to say, but I did not know the word for bristles so I said 'your *cerdos color de naranjas* (oranges) are very like an English breed called *el Tamworth*'. 'Do you grow many oranges in England?' he asked; I said we did not but that we grew pears and apples *muy rico*, that the *manzana* Cox was the *mas rico* apple in the world.

After passing through Torreperogil the road joined the main road from Albacete to Jaén, and I had to ride along it in the growing dusk with lorries flying past, so I held out a white handkerchief in my left hand so as to avoid being run into from behind. We found a track which cut off the last loop in the road and entered Ubeda at the lower end, through the horseshoe arch of the Moorish gate of the Rosal. The poor Marquesa was so weary she tried to turn into one house after another, hoping it might be the *posada*. The usual children attached themselves to us and I asked them to lead the way to the government *Parador* about which I had heard so much from Annie. It seemed an age before we reached it only to be told that there were no stables. A young man now joined our procession, attracted by the charms of the Marquesa, not by mine. I learnt later that he had done his military service in the Sevillian cavalry and had a passion for horses. He said he knew of a *posada*, so along we went and banged on the locked double doors loud and long. When the landlady at last appeared it was to say that she and her husband were going away first thing in the morning so they could not take anybody in. I was leading the Marquesa by this time and could hardly put one foot before another, nor could she, for having gone so much out of our way we could not have covered much less than sixty kilometres since leaving Cazorla. If only somebody would provide us with a stable I would willingly have slept in the loft, or in a manger like George Borrow so often did, or on the cobbles beside the muleteers. We were now directed to a second *posada* but the landlord had no *paja*! I was too desperate to laugh. I turned to the young man and commanded: 'Take me to the barracks of the *Guardia Civil*!' So there we went and it seemed like a five-kilometre walk right to the outskirts of the town and it turned out to be enormous, as Ubeda is a big training centre. I asked to see the Colonel and implored him to stable the poor Marquesa. He was very sympathetic but feared this was impossible and told me of yet a third *posada* which he knew had plenty of *cebada y paja*. I began inwardly to curse the religious mania which had brought me here. How could I walk back through the town when my mare and I were on the point of collapse? Then my companion made a suggestion: his father-in-law lived in the next street and had a stable, he would see if we could stay there. So there we went and it turned out to be a tiny house at the end of a wide untidy unpaved street called by the grand name of the *Avenida del 18 julio*. The Señor was out and the Señora in Barcelona staying with a married daughter, but three of their five daughters were sitting round their cosy-table in the little sitting-room sewing and knitting and tailoring. The eldest was called Paquita, a fine great girl, and was the wife of Miguel, my guide and benefactor. She said she was sure her father would take us in and in the meantime allowed the Marquesa to be put into the stable and fed. Miguel led her in through the front door, across the cobbled hall and out into a tiny yard at the back where two ewes, three lambs, two huge tame rabbits, seven hens and a cockerel lived. To the left of this yard there was a small stable occupied by an old black pack-pony and a collie-like bitch lying in a rush basket suckling a large creamy woolly ball, her puppy Tarzan. The Marquesa was tied up alongside the black pony and having drunk her fill of water earlier on at a *fuente* she was given a big feed which she dived straight into in spite of her great fatigue. A good doer is the greatest blessing on a ride of this kind: an animal that will go on eating in spite of strange stables and strange company.

The Esposito family

The Marquesa fed, but I felt too exhausted to make conversation for perhaps two hours before supper. I said I would go to the *Parador* but Miguel said it was twenty minutes' walk away so he took me to a nearby hotel and left me there. It was exactly eight o'clock and dinner did not start until nine so I sat in the gloomy sitting-room with orange walls and dim lights at a cosy-table which wasn't cosy because the ashes in the *brasero* were cold, until the waiter came and announced dinner which was produced in an icy room with a one-bar electric stove to heat the guests. Thank God I had a table to myself. I had broth, little fish rissoles, and a slice of veal with cabbage, and made myself drink a glass of very nasty sour wine as a tonic.

When I got back to the *Avenida del 18 julio*, the girl's father had returned. He eyed me with slight suspicion and said: 'There are many bad people about: have you any identification papers with you?' I dived into my *alforjas*, found the plastic sponge-bag and produced my passport and the Marquesa's identity paper, both of which he perused carefully for some minutes. Then he looked up and smiled and said I was welcome to stay in his house.

Miguel and Paquita had a furnished room of their own in a house two streets away, but they had all their meals at her parents' because Paquita was the best cook in the family and very good she proved to be. Her younger sisters Trini, aged twenty (engaged to a motor mechanic named Pepe, employed by a local 'bus company) and Pepita aged eighteen, lived at home. The latter asked me if I minded sharing a bedroom with herself and her sister or would I prefer to have a bed brought down into the sitting-room? I said I would be delighted to share so she took me upstairs to her bedroom where she had made up a narrow single bed with nice clean sheets. It was near the glassless window and a tall chest-of-drawers divided it from a slightly wider bed in which the two sisters slept.

On the walls hung four oleographs of ladies in brightly coloured 1920's dresses. I got into bed first and by the time the girls came up I must have been fast asleep for I never heard another sound till morning when Señor Esposito called up to the girls at eight o'clock and told them to get busy with the housework.

FRIDAY, NOVEMBER 24. *Feast of San Juan de la Cruz*

To-day I had such an orgy of spiritual, gastronomic and aesthetic delights as to make all the trials of yesterday worth while.

First, Mass in my parish church of St Isidoro; then a wonderful breakfast at the *Parador* with Russian tea, real toast, the first butter I have tasted since leaving Illora, peach jam, and a delicious Ubeda variation on the theme of the Bath bun; then High Mass at the Carmelite Church of San Miguel with a full choir of friars singing in four parts: but the trebles, local boys I presume, sang with *cante jondo* methods of voice production which made the harmony sound odd and I wondered what an English Cathedral choirmaster would have thought of it.

This liturgical feast of St John of the Cross (he actually died of erysipelas in the Carmelite Monastery of Ubeda on December 12, 1591) is evidently a highbrow as opposed to a popular fiesta. No fireworks were let off at the elevation and the big congregation was obviously drawn largely from the professional class, most people being well-dressed and following the Mass in their Missals. The moving sermon on the Divine Doctrine of St John was preached by a friar from Granada and lasted for thirty-five minutes.

The Church of San Miguel adjoins the monastery and was built in 1921: an uninspired essay in characterless classical. A real 1920's touch is the square sanctuary with hideous green tesserae lining the walls to half-way up their height and looking like shagreen. On the altar, in place of the customary Crucifix, there is a highly polished brass cross with a huge white metal host nailed onto it in place of the human figure of Our Lord. I found the whole modernistic conception of this sanctuary far more disturbing in its ugliness than rows of indifferent plaster saints, but was delighted to read a notice at the west end of the nave asking for contributions for a new retablo.

When the Mass was over we all trooped next door to the baroque oratory of San Juan to kiss a relic of the saint. This was built in the early seventeenth century over the site of the cell in which he died. In the choir there are four modern frescoes of scenes from his life and writings by Palma Burgos of Malaga; but I much preferred the inspired recumbent effigy by the same artist executed in 1959 and lying on the spot where San Juan died in the odour of sanctity. I asked where the actual body reposes and was told that it had been stolen and secretly removed to Segovia in 1593 and put in the cathedral there. I learnt later that this incident gave Cervantes the idea for Don Quixote's adventure with the corpse.* Having done my homework diligently I had got as far as that and was now rapidly on the way to becoming a Cervantean bore.

Ubeda gives the lie to people who tell you that there is nothing much to see in the south of Spain; that all the good architecture is in the north. Well, you could spend a month in Seville alone sightseeing incessantly; then there is Granada, Cordoba, Ronda, Jaén, Baeza, Ubeda, all stuffed full of marvellous Moorish, Gothic, Mudejar, Renaissance, Baroque and Rococo monuments. I bought the local guide to Ubeda and spent the next three days wallowing in aesthetic delights. Now that my memory has gone I cannot attempt to mug up Spanish art history but I no longer get annoyed if I don't know all about the architects and sculptors mentioned in guide books. I

* Cervantes: *op. cit.*, Book III, ch. v.

simply enjoy their works and cease to worry about my ignorance. It is the most care-free method of sightseeing. For this reason I do not propose to catalogue everything I saw in Ubeda and to copy a lot of names and dates out of the guide which any traveller can buy for himself on arrival. I will only say that it is the Spanish Montepulciano with palaces of the high renaissance round every corner and the San Salvador standing in the place of the Madonna di San Biagio.

One of the finest palaces, built round a large patio, was converted into a Government *Parador* before the war, but as I found to my sorrow the night before, they had also converted the stables. I returned there for luncheon which was excellent, but rejoiced that I was not actually staying in it because the central heating was up to American standards.

Back to the Carmelite church for Benediction which was packed out and I stood behind a pillar until some kind people squashed closer together to make room for me at the end of their pew. Another half-hour sermon, this time on the subject of death and how St John had welcomed it. I was understanding more of every sermon I heard, and delivered as they were in good Castillian there was no better language practice.

When I got back to the Esposito's house I found that the Señora had returned from Barcelona with her little grand-daughter Maria, aged five. Nine of us sat round a nice hot cosy-table to supper of loaves and fishes and olives and melon, all of which we ate with our fingers and our *navajas*. Afterwards I attempted to write letters with the usual interruptions: neighbours dropping in, the *porrón* being passed round, everyone wanting to know about the cost of living in England and Maria needing to be entertained. At last I gave up the struggle and took on the latter duty myself. My dragons were getting better and fiercer with all the practice I was getting: they were covered with scales and horns and with the aid of a red biro they breathed real flames. The Spaniards think it very unkind to send children to bed before the grown-ups and everywhere I have been it is the custom for all of them, toddlers to teenagers, to stay up until past midnight and often to sleep on till after ten the next day. The official hour for schools to start is 10 a.m. Maria slept in our dormitory between her Aunts Trini and Pepita and I again slept like a log after one of the most self-indulgent days of my life.

SATURDAY, NOVEMBER 25

After another lovely breakfast at the *Parador* I wandered round the *mercado municipal* where I bought a toy horse for Maria, a kilo of carrots for the real horses, and some oranges and bananas for us. A one-toothed old girl appeared and asked if I would like to see a very old house. I followed her down two narrow straight streets, through a door into a small patio surrounded by two storeys of wooden arches. All the floors were uneven and you got a very Tudor feeling with one room leading into another. She lived in two rooms on the first floor with very little furniture and an open fire of smouldering *paja*. She told me she had no children and that her husband had died many years ago. I insisted on giving her a 25-*peseta* piece though she was no beggar and would have borne me no resentment had I gone off and given her nothing.

Miguel, the ex-cavalryman, exercised the Marquesa for me after she had had a full day's rest. He then spent the afternoon cleaning my tack and boots, which he did quite beautifully with a tin of *grasa de caballo* (horse grease) which I had bought at his request. He thought it really was made of horse fat. It reminded me of Ford's recipe for man grease, *unto del hombre*, which he got from a Doctor in Seville and which was said to be the best possible unguent for healing scars: 'Take a man in full health who has just been killed, the fresher the better, pare off the fat round the heart, melt it over a slow fire, clarify, and put it away in a cool place for use.' Ford adds that 'the multitudinous church ceremonies and holidays in Spain, which bring crowds together, combined with the sun, wine and women, have always ensured a supply of fine subjects.'

It having rained all the morning the sun came out in fits and starts in the afternoon, so I went and did some photography and a lot of sightseeing. Found the church of Santo Domingo, formerly a mosque, and most astonishing of all I found the woman who kept the key and who let me in through the delicate plateresque south door. The inside was gutted in the civil war but there is a well-preserved and magnificent *mudejar* (name given to the Moorish-Gothic mixture style) wooden ceiling of square and hexagonal panels.

Next I found the lady custodian of San Lorenzo which was also gutted and without a good ceiling, but still retaining a pretty west gallery. This church is used as a coach house for *andas*, the chariots which carry the *pasos* (figures of Our Lord and Our Lady and the saints) in religious processions, including the beaten silver one belonging to Our Lady of Guadalupe who comes to Ubeda from her nearby sierra seat for three or four months each summer. This and the gilded wood baroque chariots standing beside it are all protected from the dust by close-fitting check gingham covers and present a strange spectacle in this desolate church.

I then walked about a mile to the north-east of the town to see St Nicholas which, thank God, is ungutted. It has a late Gothic south door reminiscent of French flamboyant, and a classical north door, 1566, by Andrés de Valdevira, the architect of the San Salvador. I mention this name because he was apparently one of the leading Spanish architects of the sixteenth century, though I confess I had not previously heard of him. Fourteenth-century Gothic interior with the renaissance chapel of Deán Ortega containing the most beautiful *verja* I have yet seen. *Verjas* are wrought-iron screens with figures worked into the pattern and painted on both sides. They are one of the great surprises which Spain holds for newcomers to her architecture.

On the other side of the nave of St Nicholas there is another great surprise: seated in a chapel at a wooden E-shaped table (minus the centre stroke) are life-sized highly coloured plaster figures of our Lord and the twelve Apostles at the Last Supper, with Judas furtively slinking away clutching his money-bag. The *párroco*, whom I found in the sacristy, told me that this *paso* (which is taken out on Maundy Thursday) was modelled five years ago in Cordoba by a certain Ruiz Olmas. It is much admired by the townspeople.

Back in my adopted home I found there were squids for supper in the usual browny yellow sauce. 'The English', says Ford, 'have but one sauce, melted butter, and a hundred different religions: whereas in orthodox Spain there is but one of each . . . so to change this sauce would be little short of heresy.'

With the squids we had an excellent salad of cos lettuce, sliced onions and pimientos. The main dish was put in the middle of the cosy-table and we all ate out of it with our spoons and without plates. The Spaniards drink a lot of water between meals straight out of the amphora but never with their meals. Neither do they always drink wine, presumably because it is not so plentiful here as in France or Italy as there seem to be far fewer vineyards.

SUNDAY, NOVEMBER 26

Pepita, the youngest daughter of the house, aged eighteen, belongs to a religious sisterhood which places her under the obligation to receive Holy Communion every Sunday, so she came to Mass with me in our parish church where it always starts dead on time. I became very fond of San Isidoro: it is Gothic outside and completely renaissance within. There is a shallow cupola over the chancel with carvings of the four evangelists in the spandrels; otherwise very little decoration, as it was sacked in 1936 when the retablo, organ and statues were destroyed.

The parish priest said Mass at the High Altar and one of his curates preached a long sermon during the offertory, through the Sanctus and right up to the Consecration. He knelt for this, then got up again and continued until the celebrant's communion when he announced in a loud voice: '*Ahora se va a comulgar.*' (Now we will receive Holy Communion.) He walked across to the Blessed Sacrament chapel where we all knelt and recited the *confiteor*, as in the old order of Mass. I am not a liturgical snob but I did find this preaching technique very distracting as I like to follow Mass in my Missal. However, I had to give up the battle and concentrate on the sermon which was riveting, on the subject of parents' duties towards their children. The curate told a story about a woman who had lost one of her hens and went from one neighbour to another to enquire if any of them had seen it. Late that night she was still looking for it when she met St John Chrysostom and asked him if he had seen a small white hen straying about the streets.

'You ask me about a chicken, Madam,' he replied, 'and pray tell me where is your nineteen-year-old daughter?'

'Oh, I don't know! She is out with her young man I suppose.'

'And you allow your daughter to tread the road to hell with her young man while you spend all these hours searching for a hen!'

On the way home from Mass Pepita and I called in to see Paquita who was still in bed, though Miguel had got up and gone out. They had a bed sitting-room in what appeared to be a tenement house, and they shared a kitchen with four other tenants. The room was very large and clean and furnished with a modern suite including a wardrobe. They had only been married three months and I was made to look at all the wedding presents and right through the trousseau which consisted chiefly of a good selection of nightgowns.

When we got home there was no sign of any breakfast. No one can accuse the Spaniards of being the slaves of early morning cups of tea. Instead we marched off to the covered market carrying a basket each. It was seething with people and all the salesmen were shouting at the tops of their voices. Outside on the pavement a man was selling dried rosemary and lavender and thyme from the mountains. Rosemary is often burnt on the *brasero* which fills the room with a delicious scent and reminds one of the practice of London hostesses who burn expensive essence in an iron spoon before a smart luncheon party.

The fish market consisted of two rows of stalls facing one another with fresh sardines, hake, squids, prawns, bream, mussels and fresh anchovies. Pepita bought some of the latter for her father's breakfast. The fruit and vegetable market displayed apples, oranges, lemons, tomatoes, tangerines, bananas, onions, garlic, globe artichokes, French beans, leeks, carrots, very long radishes, spinach-beat, pimientos, grapes and large black acorns. Pepita bought some artichokes because I told her how much I liked them, and some French beans and onions and potatoes. I bought some bananas and some round flat buns with sugar on top which I thought we could eat for breakfast as I did not fancy a bowl of slops.

It was after ten when we got home again and nearer eleven when we at last broke our fast. Señor Esposito and Miguel had fried fresh anchovies; I ate two of my buns dry with barley coffee and the others broke up their buns and poured coffee over them and ate slops for which the Latin races appear to have a passion. We were all up in the kitchen together, some standing, some sitting, while little Pilila, a small tame hen, walked about the floor picking up my bun crumbs and hopping on and off the window-sill. Paquita told me that the other hens used to peck her because she was undersized, so she brought her upstairs and made a pet of her. Who says Spaniards are unkind to animals?

Pepita begged me to accompany her and Maria to the *Guardia Civil* barracks after breakfast where there was a jamboree in progress starting with Mass in the huge and extremely draughty riding school. About five hundred men stood at attention throughout except at the elevation when they knelt as one man and the band played the national anthem. After Mass all the officers kissed the colours, then there was a parade outside and a march past. The Colonel I had met on my first night in Ubeda took the salute.

I had been persuaded to stay over Sunday with the promise that if I did they would kill the 'fatted calf', in my honour. On returning from the *Guardia Civil* celebrations I sat down to write letters at a narrow table against the kitchen wall when in marched my host carrying a colossal tame rabbit by the ears. Up till now it had lived happily in the yard with a slightly smaller friend. Señor Esposito beamed all over as he drew a finger across his throat, making a guttural sound foreshadowing what was about to happen. I supposed that he had brought it up to show me that it was a genuine rabbit and not a cat which was going into the *olla* and that he would then take it back into the yard where he would kill and skin it. Not at all. He handed it to Paquita, who, cool as a cucumber, drew out her *navaja* and slit its

throat. It closed its eyes as I closed mine and said a prayer
that it might die quickly as I always do when killing a
hen. Its life-blood poured out into an enamel basin and
little five-year-old Maria roared with laughter while the
cat made horrible and vicious noises, impatient to devour the intestines. I had witnessed a sacrifice on the
hearth, a sacrifice that was being offered for me as the
guest of honour.

It appears to be an ancient tradition to kill and cook an
animal in front of the guest so that he can be certain that
no foul joke is being played on him. Gina, my Italian
maid, told me that in her Calabrian village, if you wanted
to get even with an enemy, you pretended to make up
your quarrel and invited him to dinner to eat a rabbit
stew. At the end of the meal you brought in the cat's
head and paws on a plate.

Burckhardt describes a more sinister meal in the district of Aquapendente when a peasant killed a boy with
a knife and served up the liver to his father.* And this
was the same tradition as the macabre feast described
by Herodotus in which King Astyages asked his courtier
Harpagus how he had enjoyed his repast? 'Excessively'
was the reply, whereupon a basket was brought in containing the head and hands and feet of his son.†

While some onions were frying in oil in an outsize
pan Paquita paunched, skinned and jointed the rabbit
with professional skill. Having killed, plucked and drawn
many hundreds of ducks, geese and chickens in my
time I did not feel squeamish about this procedure. Half
the meat was then put to fry in the pan and the pieces
were turned over as in the traditions of the best cookery.
Then about one and a half pounds of rice was added,
some sliced potatoes, three or four bay leaves, a little

* Jacob Burckhardt: *The Civilization of the Renaissance*, Part VI, Section on
Morality and Immorality (Phaidon).
† Rawlinson's *Herodotus*, Book I, par. 119 (John Murray, 1862).

pimiento powder and several cloves of garlic pounded together with parsley in a small brass mortar. Paquita then poured on enough cold water (I should have used boiling) to cover the contents of the pan and when it had come to the boil she added the baby globe artichokes and French beans and let everything simmer together for half an hour.

Sunday lunch was ready by 3.30 p.m. and a great feast it was. The contents of the huge black frying-pan were turned out into an equally huge earthenware bowl and we all sat round the cosy-table and dug into it with our spoons and spiked bits of rabbit with our *navajas* and gnawed the meat off the bones, and the *porrón* went round and round and I brought the house down by pouring the wine up my nose instead of down my throat. The little artichokes were marvellous: whilst most things are tough in Spain, artichokes are wonderfully tender and you can eat the whole thing, leaves, choke and all. In other countries you eat the leaves, carefully cut out the choke and gobble up the *fond*.

After luncheon the only washing up there was to do was the earthenware bowl and the spoons. Paquita and Miguel then went home, Trini and Pepita went upstairs to dress for the Sunday afternoon promenade, Señor Esposito went to sleep at the cosy-table with his head resting on his folded arms, I wrote my diary, and a friend came in and talked to the Señora about their respective insides and the insides of their neighbours. Maria had gone home with her parents before lunch so there would be only three of us in the dormitory to-night.

Later I went out to make a final attempt to see inside the Trinidad church, which up till now had defied all my ingenuity in running the sacristan to earth. On the way I walked into the *patio* of the enormous sixteenth-century hospital of Santiago, again by Andrés de Valdevira, and

Escorialesque in its classical severity, and through into the chapel where the Blessed Sacrament was exposed in front of yards and yards of pleated pale blue nylon—the retablo having been inevitably destroyed in 1936. The only reason why I was now able to get into the Trinidad was because it was open for a brief half-hour for evening Mass, but being crowded out it was impossible to walk around. However the interior was not nearly so exciting as the baroque west door had led me to believe and contained no plasterwork. At the end of the nave there was a large gilt *andas* bearing a life-size *paso* figure of Our Lord on a donkey which is taken round the town in the Palm Sunday procession.

Supper consisted of the remaining half of the rabbit stewed with more rice and vegetables. Odd that they did not keep this till next day as we had already had one excellent meat meal; but Spaniards seem determined to eat all kinds of meat on the same day as it is killed. The Tonsen-Ryes had told me that the Duke's servants never killed the turkey until Christmas morning. We discussed labour problems: both Miguel and Señor Esposito are day-labourers and never get hired in wet weather. But they have a smallholding which provides them with a certain amount of work and food. The remainder of the family income is made up chiefly by Trini who is a trained tailoress and makes suits for several men in the neighbourhood. How I wish that Gandhi's ideal could be realised in Spain more completely than it has been in India! A great number of small industries have been set up in rural Andalusia since the civil war: potteries, factories for esparto grass products, peach canning factories and olive oil presses. If only these and more like them could provide full employment I think the people would be happier than with the installation of heavy industries.

A parish priest

To-day, whatever the weather, I had to descend into
the glorious valley of the beastly Guadalquivir. Went to
my last Mass at St Isidoro, my last breakfast at the
Parador, and for a last look round Ubeda's number one
church, the San Salvador. Here I met the *párroco* who
was very friendly and full of information. He refused to
take the money I proffered him towards the restoration
of the badly damaged interior, saying that this was being
carried out entirely at the expense of the Duchess of
Medinaceli of Seville (her *mudejar* palace there, known as
the *Casa del Pilato*, is one of the great sights of Spain).

The *párroco* asked me if I had noticed how peaceful the
countryside was? I said, 'Yes, and the Andalusians are all
so nice that I believe they are untouched by original sin.'
He laughed and then spoke seriously about Franco and
said he was *un santo* and that he never took a big decision
without spending the night in prayer before the Blessed
Sacrament; that Señora Franco once came to Ubeda for
Holy Week but that her husband couldn't come as he
always spent it in retreat. He went on to tell me that the
civil war had been like the Roman persecutions in early
Christian times: that he had only escaped with his life
because he ran (and still runs) a school for poor boys. He
hid three Carmelite friars in his house for some time and
knew of two others who died as the result of being tor-
tured. He then showed me round the church, pointing
out the damage that the Reds had done: the first chapel
on the left as you enter by the west door had been used as
a kitchen, wood for the fire being provided by the
chopped-up images from other chapels; the treasure from
the sacristy had all been stolen, the vaults desecrated, the
Pedro Berruguete bas-reliefs of carved wood torn down
from the choir (they are at present stacked in the sacristy
awaiting restoration), and a small marble statue of the

infant St John the Baptist, attributed to Michelangelo, had been hammered into fragments. You can still see a hand and a few other odd bits in the sacristy cupboard.

On my way home I met Miguel out on the Marquesa. Told him I wanted to set off soon and he said he was just riding along to show the mare to his father and would then return to the *Avenida del 18 julio*. I went to the saddler's and bought a new *bota* to take back to England as a present for my husband, then went to a bar and had it half filled with cheap brandy. This is supposed to 'break it in'. I then returned to pack my *alforjas* and await the arrival of the horse-mad Miguel. Watched Paquita and her mother making *migas*, not the sort made by Doña Encarna in the infernal regions, but the more usual variety (described by Ford) consisting of breadcrumbs and garlic fried in oil, with water added. A very different meal from our Sunday feast. I now got horse as opposed to train fever because Miguel took so long in coming, and feared the Marquesa would be exhausted before we set out. He did not return for nearly an hour, after which we all bade one another a fond farewell with promises of letters and photographs. For four nights I had slept in the little house at the end of the avenue: I had become an adopted member of the family, coming and going as I pleased, and been made to feel completely at home. A sacrifice had been offered for me on the sacred hearth and I had been royally fed; so had the Marquesa who had shared the stable of the humble black pony after being refused at inn after inn: and when I took leave of my friends Señor Esposito only wanted to charge me for the mare's barley!

I rode down an untarred lane past some huge medieval walls and leaving the Granada gate on my left, plunged into the olive groves below the town. I had planned to go to a little mountain *pueblo* called Bedmar on the far side of the valley but it was a foregone conclusion that I would get lost because I was coming within the sphere of influence of my arch-enemy, the wicked river Guadalquivir. After a sunny morning the sky was now clouding over and as I sat on a grassy bank eating hard-boiled eggs and bread and cheese and apples and chocolate, it started to rain. I put on my black oilskin and rode on along winding tracks where it was difficult to keep my bearings. Eventually we came to a road which led past a brand new *pueblo*, a government agricultural settlement, with church and school which I longed to go and have a look round but was deterred by the now heavy rain. The river, for which I was making, would show itself when I was on high ground but, as soon as I advanced towards it, would disappear. In the end the road led to a bridge over my persecutor, which was not the one I had planned to cross at all but some fourteen kilometres east of it. We also went over the same railway track which we had crossed further south near Pedro Martinez. I found our whereabouts on my now rapidly disintegrating maps and saw that it would be impossible to reach Bedmar before night, so decided on Jódar. The river sprites took great delight in concealing a broad grassy track away to our left which ran parallel to the tarred road, and in guiding us along the latter. On and on for nine kilometres we jogged in the pouring rain and when I turned round to look back across the valley the whole of the Baeza–Ubeda ridge was lost in a dark night of cloud.

We rode into the long narrow sierra-framed *pueblo* of Jódar as the sun set in a stormy sky, and found a perfectly situated *posada* in the *plaza* with a renaissance church on one side and, opposite, a *fuente* for the Marquesa and a café for me. I dismounted and led her into the covered cobbled yard through enormous double doors, out into an open yard beyond on the far side of which were the largest *posada* stables I have ever seen. I counted 106 mangers round the walls, all untenanted bar those used by the Marquesa and two donkeys. There were no pigs, but there were ten hens and a cock. I went out to buy barley as they had none at the inn and found the shop in the main street. The mare's corn was now costing me five shillings a day, the usual price being five *pesetas* a kilo and her ration having been raised to eight kilos a day since the terrible disclosure of the Quesada pig scales.

I called on the *párroco* to find out the times of the services. He was a sweet old priest called Don Antonio, short and fat and bald with a beaming smile on his face. Asked his advice about riding to the shrine of the Virgin of Fuensanta near Huelma where I proposed to proceed next day. He told me I must be certain to visit another shrine, the *Santuario de la Virgen de Cuadro* near Bedmar (where I was meant to be that night), before going to Fuensanta, but he did not think I could see them both in a day as the sierras between them were very wild and steep and he thought I ought to go by the main road. He then directed me to the house of the *praticante*, Don Rafael, four doors away from the presbytery, because my throat was a bit sore again so I had decided to have another injection. It was given as painlessly as the ones at Cazorla. Ford's chapter on Spanish doctors is one of the funniest in the *Gatherings;* but nobody need have any fears about the state of medicine or dentistry in modern Spain which is as up-to-date as in England with the same drugs in constant use. In Malaga I had to have a new crown put on a front tooth having broken one on a hard roll. The impression was taken and a plastic one made and fitted all on the same day because I told the dentist (who was dressed in white from head to foot, including his shoes) that I had booked a seat in the 'bus going to Granada. In Malaga too I had my second typhoid injection. In Cazorla my septic sinusitis was quickly diagnosed and treated, and the ingenuity of *praticantes* in giving intra-muscular injections must be experienced to be believed. I say all this because many English people are still under the misapprehension that they might die if taken ill in Spain as there cannot possibly be any competent doctors in the south of Europe.

I had been allotted a double bedroom in the *posada* with a splendid crooked washstand, some wall-pegs and two chairs. Outside my bedroom there was an abnormally wide stone landing with a large spy-hole in it for viewing people in the covered yard below. Posada architects are a very eccentric race; their plans are always asymmetrical and full of surprises.

Evening devotions were at 7 p.m. in the large church next door. This had been entirely gutted during the civil war and converted into a cinema. The vast gilt retablo in the baroque tradition covering the whole of the east wall was made in Seville nine years ago at the cost of half a million *pesetas*. Devotions began with the five joyful mysteries, then the litany of Our Lady, then a procession in which Don Antonio, wearing a black cape and preceded by a man carrying a black-and-gold banner and a boy carrying a black-and-gold umbrella (Buddhist symbol of royalty), walked down to the Holy Souls altar and intoned an extraordinary duet with the 'choir'—that is to say, one lady in the gallery who played a runny theme on the harmonium and sang *cante jondo* through her nose at the top of her voice. The effect was mesmeric and I could hardly believe my ears, but nobody else appeared to think it odd.

In the *posada* that evening I sat with the family and two other guests, photographers from Jaén, a father and son who tour round their province taking family and wedding groups. Under the cosy-table I saw a wire cage fitted over the *brasero* with clothes airing on it. On a sofa against the wall sat a spherical matriarch. She never spoke but looked vacantly through me. From time to time she beckoned to a boy who without a word would go to a sideboard and fetch a syphon of soda water. The matriarch would squirt some of this straight down her throat and up came her wind in a series of loud belches. I got the giggles but everyone else took it as a matter of course so I stopped. Fortunately one is not inclined to giggle alone for long. Between 10 and 11 p.m. my pretty landlady, big with child, produced the all too familiar supper of fried eggs swimming in oil in soup plates. And as usual I mopped up the oil with my bread.

TUESDAY, NOVEMBER 28

I had breakfast of *tortas* and a *cappucino* in the café opposite the *posada*. It was pouring with tropical rain and continued to do so until mid-day when I walked up to photograph the well-preserved Moorish castle above the church. Beyond it there was an unsuspected cave colony with the odd stone chimneys pushing up from the bowels of the earth.

Down came the rain again and when I returned to the *posada* I found a barrow full of prawns and its owner sheltering in the covered yard. I bought fifteen *pesetas* worth for my lunch, which turned out to be far more than I could eat. Forced to postpone my departure but in the late afternoon the rain stopped and the sun came out so I went for a two-hour ride following the directions given me that morning by two Civil Guards who had inevitably questioned me about my identity and purpose. They had told me there was a good track leading round a blue hill to the east of the *pueblo* called Cerro Hernando. I jogged past the cemetery on the gates of which were written the Ash Wednesday injunction: 'Remember thou O man, that dust thou art and unto dust shalt thou return.' Thought how much I would like to become Spanish dust.

Jódar

I now found the track with wide grass verges on either side which led to the bridge over the river which I had crossed yesterday. Had it not been for the evil genii I could have avoided the tarred road altogether. Without the additional weight of the *alforjas* we cantered happily for a couple of miles along the grass then turned right up a track leading through an olive grove to a white farmhouse which I had seen from the outskirts of Jódar. From here a good gravelly mule-path led round the side of the hill with marvellous views across the broad valley of the Guadalquivir to the long low ridge on the horizon where I could dimly see the towns of Baeza and Ubeda. The elusive white ribbon of the river looked so pure, but I could neither forget nor forgive that its chief delight was to lead weary travellers astray and send them far further than they needed to go.

The landscape was equalled by the skyscape of low black and silver clouds scurrying over the St John of the Cross country with great sierras, some of them powdered with snow, poking out above them. Away in the west the hidden sun sent rays of light slanting through cloud banks between which shone patches of the luminous green sky of Umbrian painting.

'Bridle Road to . . .' When I see this notice in England it has the same effect on me as Mescalin does on Mr Aldous Huxley. Here there are no such notices but you can see the bridle roads leading over the plains and the sierras in every direction and to an addict the sight is intoxicating. Every one has his weaknesses: some people run after women, others after Dukes; I run after priests and along *carriles* which, with their alluringly sinuous ways, are gravely tempting me to throw all my family duties to the wind and to go on riding along them for ever.

I thought it odd that when I returned to the *posada* at 7 p.m. my landlady's sister was scrubbing the wide stone landing, then started down the long flight of steep stone steps. I took off my very muddy jodhpur boots in the covered yard so as not to discourage her. I thought this was simply another Spanish eccentricity, a *cosa de España*, to do your housework in the evening.

My landlady cooked my supper, then did some ironing at the cosy-table until 11 p.m. She used an iron filled with charcoal and blew through a hole at one end when she wanted to increase the heat. Although there is electricity in every *pueblo* nobody seems to have any power points. I wanted to write letters but three men sitting at the cosy-table kept talking to me so I said: 'Do you think Antonio is the best bullfighter living to-day?' This was a brilliant ruse as it got all three of them talking and arguing furiously so that I might not have been there. They were still hard at it describing the memorable passes of their champions when I went to bed after midnight.

I slept for about two hours and then woke and heard excited voices talking on the great landing and footsteps hurrying up and down the stone stairs. Sleep was no longer possible so I went on with my letters, and slowly the obvious truth dawned upon me: my young landlady was having her first baby two rooms away from mine. That was why her sister had so scrupulously scrubbed the *posada* from top to bottom last night!

On my way to Mass I asked if all was well and learned that little Sabelita was born at 3.15 a.m. with the help of a midwife after only two hours of labour. I tiptoed into the bedroom and there was a beautiful little baby girl lying beside her radiant young mother. I promised to make them my intention at Mass.

WEDNESDAY, NOVEMBER 29

I looked all over the *Mercado Municipal* for flowers with which to bunch the new mother but there were none

to be had: all the summer ones were over and there was
no demand for forced ones, so I bought her some grapes
and a box of chocolates.

The spherical soda-water-drinking matriarch was now
transformed by grandmotherhood into a laughing joking
old girl. Whereas before the happy event she had just
sat and stared into space she now bustled about the kitchen and the yard talking at a great rate and asking
me to take her with me on the Marquesa.

After mounting in the covered yard by means of the
customary chair I set off for the *cuadro* shrine. Out at the
far end of the long main street I found a narrow path
through the olive trees. I had made friends with the
postmaster in the café who had given me excellent directions for getting to the sanctuary. I had to turn left by
a ruined house which I found very easily and follow the
track which would lead me to the sanctuary. It was my
favourite sort of bridle road through a hilly cultivated
valley completely surrounded by sierras which got deeper
blue as they reached into the distance. Oh, the healing
silence of Spain! It is like lanolin being rubbed into your
soul.

The track led down into a gully where it almost petered
out, but with my well-trained eye for droppings I noticed
some on the far side and followed them up and onto the
track again. We came to the edge of a ravine with a
mountain torrent rushing down it through the most
beautiful of all the Grimm's fairy-tale mills of Spain, and
behind the mill rose a giant Patinir crag with a tiny toy
watch-tower perched on the top. To the right of the crag
was the sanctuary with the church and sacristan's house
all jumbled up together and a patio enclosed by whitewashed walls to one side.

I got off and led the Marquesa down the precipitous
rock path to the mill and up the other side and into the
courtyard where I tied her up to a small tree and entered

The Virgen de Cuadro

the little church of the *Santisima Virgen de Cuadro, Patrona de Bedmar*. It had the date of 1616 on the south wall and was the prettiest country church I have seen in Andalusia: completely unrestored with a west choir gallery supported by two doric columns, a coved ceiling, and bands of grey and white raised plasterwork in strap patterns round the walls of the nave. Behind the altar, and protected by a glass screen, stood the little Virgin in her stiff brocade dress with wax flowers banked up round her feet. Having recited a decade or two of the rosary I rode away from this lost sierra shrine leaving the sacristan's children playing at churches: on a large flat stone they had built an altar and laid a yellow member of the compositae family upon it which looked like ragwort but wasn't.

Down at the mill I asked an old boy if a certain path on the other side of the gorge led to Fuensanta. He said that it did but that it was a *camin muy malo* and he did not think I should ever find my way there and I had much better go round by the road. This was a challenge and I rode straight up the said path for a hundred yards when a mule appeared from the opposite direction heavily laden with pinewood. It is an unwritten law of the sierras that the loaded pack animal has the right of way so I had to turn back, passing was out of the question as the path was very narrow. I asked the muleteer if many more animals were coming down from the mountains and he said that men and beasts would be descending all the afternoon so that it would be impossible to ride that way to Fuensanta to-day. This was the only traffic problem I encountered on my tour. Frustrated, I sat down and ate my lunch and turned the Marquesa loose to eat her favourite *celvero* weed, there being very little grass. While we were both munching happily I counted twenty-seven mules, ponies and donkeys walking down the path towards Jódar with their loads of winter fuel. Consulted my small pieces of torn map and decided we would make for a *pueblo* called Belmez de la Moraleda in the Sierra de Magina for the night and proceed from there to Fuensanta.

We jogged back towards the *carretera* and on the way met two ploughmen enjoying their siesta beneath an olive tree. I asked if there was a short cut over the mountains to Belmez and one of the men said that there was and that if I turned to the right and followed the track up the mountain and then kept always to the left, I would cut off many kilometres. So up we went, zig-zagging among the little holly oaks and broom and gorse and daphne and rosemary, until we got very high and saw the tarred road a long way below us in a narrow valley. I felt triumphant having beaten it so thoroughly this time for we had left the Guadalquivir far behind and were no longer subject to its confounding influence. But the sky had clouded over and along came the rain and on went my hooded oilskin but not, alas, my yellow sou'wester which I had lost the day before on Cerro Hernando, so that I had to keep on my very battered Sevillian hat and tip my head forward from time to time to let the water pour off its wide grey brim. I began to get vertigo because the track had narrowed to a goat path and the mountain fell away so steeply to our left. Started on the joyful mysteries which kept me from panicking, but having plonked my mind upon Botticelli's Annunciation in the Uffizi it soon faded out and I found myself reciting the Hail Mary's while meditating on whether the scrub of the mountainside was strong enough to arrest the Marquesa and me in our fall. We came to a beautiful grass-covered saddle in the rocks and my sense of direction told me that we should cross over this and descend on the far side. But it fell away in a precipice at our feet which disappeared into an abyss of black cloud with sinister crags poking out here and there: another dream of the romantic painters which I would rather gaze upon in the canvasses of Fuseli and John Martin than in real life. Then I remembered the directions of the ploughman: 'Always to the left,' so I returned to the goat path which for the past hour had had no droppings of any sort upon it but which was just distinguishable winding in and out of the rocks and shrubs. If a bank of cloud chose to descend on our sierra we were done. I had now got to the sorrowful mysteries—El Greco's Agony in the National Gallery—but was actually meditating on plans for the night should the mist make further progress impossible. It was wet but it was not cold. I would loosen the Marquesa's girth and leave the saddle on for warmth for she was not accustomed to lying out. There was plenty of *celvero* for her supper and she had had a good drink before lunch at the mill. I would remove her bridle and tie her to a holly oak by the halter rope so as to prevent her from walking over a precipice in the dark. My outsize black oilskin would afford me ample protection if I treated it like a tent and I could lie on the sheepskin saddle cover. I had quite a big piece of bread left over from lunch, a lemon, and some almonds and raisins. If it were to get cold in the night I could force some of the filthy *bota* brandy down my throat and create an interior fire. So, on the whole, our prospects were not all that bad. The great thing would be to remain stationary if enveloped in a thick mountain mist as this was no *patrimonio forestal* track that we were following as on the Sierra de Cazorla but a scatter-brain goat path which in places was completely obliterated so little did it appear to be used. At what seemed to be the highest point in our ride we suddenly came upon two misty blue rosemary bushes in full bloom. They were so beautiful up there on the wild wet mountain and they filled me with pious thoughts about Maria Rosa Mystica which were all too soon replaced by others associating rosemary with the dead: '*A l'entour de sa tombe, romarin l'on planta.*' With considerable difficulty I climbed out of the saddle, becoming entangled in my long mackintosh, and broke off a sprig which I subsequently pressed in Vol. I of *Don Quixote* and later transferred to my Missal.

We rode on in pouring rain with black clouds sitting low on the peaks to the right and left of us but none descended on ours, *gracias a la Virgen tan milagrosa de Cuadro*. Then mingling with the raindrops came the faint tinkling of sheep bells, so I knew that a farm was not far off. The track descended very steeply so that we literally slid through the flock of sheep and goats who were nibbling the usual invisible grass growing on what appeared to me to be bare rock. Then we saw the little farmhouse at the bottom and cut across country through rosemary bushes and lavender to reach it. There was no one about to ask the way, so I consulted my ragged map and found that the mountain we had just crossed was most suitably named the *Sierra de la Cruz* (a northeastern spur of the great Sierra de Magina), that we had descended into the valley of the river Jandula, had taken a very successful short cut, beaten the metalled road completely, and now had roughly ten kilometres of unmetalled road to go along through a winding gloomy gorge in order to reach the *pueblo* I had selected.

At stormy dusk I rode the Marquesa into the mountain village of Belmez de la Moraleda with its lights shining in darkness and another little *pueblo*, Solera, glimmering out of an inky black sierra far away across the valley. A vast troupe of children escorted us to the tiny *posada*. The stable was approached through the living-room across a strip of cobbles in the stone paved floor; a cobbled ramp led down and down into cavernous depths and I should not have been a bit surprised to have seen the Holy Family sitting at the bottom. I tied the Marquesa to a peg and went on my eternal quest for barley. When the manger was well stocked with *paja y cebada* I asked to see my room and was led up a very narrow, winding, uneven stone staircase at the top of which, to the left of the passage, there was a small single bedroom with a steep stone step leading down to it. Every time I entered my bedroom during my two nights stay in Belmez I fell headlong into it without exception.

All the children of the *pueblo* were waiting for me as I left the *posada* to attend evening devotions. Thought I could shake them off by seeking sanctuary in church. Not at all. Benediction was in progress and I slipped into the back where there were three or four empty pews. These were immediately filled up with children and the ones in front sat on the kneelers with their backs to the Blessed Sacrament and stared at me. It was sacrilegious on their part to look at me instead of at God and I made signs to them to turn round of which they took not the slightest notice. The rest of the children stared at me from the open church door which was eventually shut by an angry man only to be burst open again a few moments later by the curious crowd.

After these disturbed devotions I went and asked the priest the time of Mass next morning. I hoped it would be nice and early as I planned to get beyond Huelma by nightfall. He said that to-morrow was the village fiesta and that there would be a sung Mass at 10 a.m. followed by a procession round the *pueblo*. I asked if St Andrew was their special patron. He said he was not but that in Belmez they paid special homage on November the 30th to Our Lord at the pillar who was known as *el Señor de la Vida*. I had noticed a painting of this subject which appeared to be a genuine primitive on the retablo behind the altar. Decided I must stay for the fiesta so went to the telegraph office and sent a wire to the Tonsen-Ryes telling them I would not return until December 3. The lady had no change and trustingly told me to come and pay next day. On my walk from the church to the office I was protected by a policeman brandishing his leather truncheon at the children who roared with laughter but gave me a wider berth.

There was a cosy-table in the corner of the living-room at the *posada* close to the open fire, so that one kept nice and warm more or less all over: but as the front door was open most of the time there were the inevitable draughts interfering with the comfort of one's upper half. Spaniards themselves are impervious to draughts. At one point there was a strong smell of burning rubber, the source of which I could not locate until my left foot felt suddenly very hot and I realised that it was resting directly on the brazier under the table so that the rubber sole of my shoe was melting away.

The only other guest was a small middle-aged man with a deep soothing voice who toured the province on a motor scooter (now stabled at the far end of the living-room) advising farmers about their olive trees and what chemical sprays to use against which pests. Mental sloth, after eight hours in the saddle and rheumatism in the knees, prevented me from making the effort of attacking chemical farming. I could not think what 'balance of nature' would be in Spanish, nor organic versus inorganic manure, and my sight was worsening after weeks of 15-watt bulbs, so that I could no longer read my dictionary at night even with my spectacles on.

We had supper at 10.45 p.m. consisting of black rubbery meat in tomato sauce. As my landlord and his wife and the chemical spray man all sat round the table with me it was difficult to slip anything to the *posada* cats. It was like playing that children's card game called 'cheating' where the object is to get rid of your cards by slipping them onto your lap without the other players noticing. I masticated and masticated which made not the slightest difference to the texture of the india-rubber in my mouth. Having swallowed several pieces whole I then had a brilliant inspiration: I put three or four bits into my mouth so as to make the conjuring trick worth while, blew my nose and transferred the meat neatly into my handkerchief, dropped my right hand down to my side and slipped the bits onto the floor where the cats loyally came to my aid as they never failed to do. The second course was a good French omelette followed by an apple.

After supper my slim young landlady, who was a *rubia* (blonde), suckled her two-month-old baby girl sitting by the fireside and we had a nice talk on breast feeding. She told me that she had had to have a Caesarian section in Jaén hospital and that she had stayed in eight days and everything was free. She had not got enough milk to satisfy the child so it was getting supplementary feeds which her husband was preparing in a saucepan simmering on hot embers. He was mad about his little Anita and prattled away to her as he held her in his arms while the mother finished feeding her with a spoon.

St Andrew's Day 1961

I got up at eight o'clock to photograph the village in the early morning light. Before going out I carried my basin of water downstairs to empty it and get some fresh in which to wash my face. The *rubia* took a wooden cover off a section of the kitchen floor and revealed a swiftly flowing stream, evidently the main drain of the village, into which I emptied my basin. There is something to be said for this method—it eliminates the curse of frozen pipes.

At 9 a.m. the church bells started to ring feverishly and a lot of rockets went off in honour of *el Señor de la Vida*. Mass being scheduled to begin at 10 a.m. I went along at 9.55 but it did not actually start until 10.40. Sat in a pew to the left of the aisle but one of the women kindly came over from the other side and reminded me that my side was reserved for men. It was stupid of me as I had already observed that this was the custom in rural Andalusia: the men and boys always sit on the left of the aisle, the women and girls on the right.

There was a lot to watch while waiting for the *Missa Cantata* to begin: Don Alberto, the *párroco*, was rushing about in a huge soutane overall (reaching to the ground) and trying to transfer the picture of Our Lord at the pillar to the gilt *andas* opposite the church door at the west end. To do this he had to remove one of the large golden wings which fitted into a slot in the back of a kneeling angel behind the high altar. He then climbed onto a chair and with great difficulty got the picture off its hooks after ten minutes of sustained and determined effort. In lifting it down, however, he gave a plaster statue of Our Lady a great biff so that she rocked in her retablo niche but fortunately did not fall. The picture was then nailed to the *andas* in readiness for the procession later on. At last the Holy Sacrifice began with the little church full to bursting point and the chief officials of the Brotherhood of Our Lord of Life grouped round the sanctuary. The choir in the west gallery consisted of five village girls caterwauling the *Missa de Angelis* accompanied by the harmonium playing not quite the same tune. But who am I to criticise church musicians? I, who in my Anglican days was dismissed from my seat at the harmonium in Baulking village church by the musical vicar who wrote to me saying that 'the disaccord between the instrument and the congregation had become so apparent as to be destructive of devotion'.

Don Alberto preached a fervent sermon on the Samaritan women and *el Señor de la Vida* at the well of Sichar: 'The water that I give him will be a spring of water within him, that flows continually to bring him everlasting life' (John iv. 14). At the elevation a volley of rockets went off, perfectly timed, and gunpowder smoke poured in at the open door completely dominating the incense fumes.

When Mass was over eight young men lifted the *andas* onto their shoulders and carried it out of the church and up and down the streets of the *pueblo* preceded by a woman carrying a red banner and all the other women in two long lines. Immediately behind the image walked Don Alberto in a white cope flanked by the chief of the Civil Guard in uniform on one side and the leader of the Brotherhood of Our Lord of Life on the other. I stepped out of line to take photographs when the procession turned down a street flooded with sunlight and the woman behind me said approvingly: 'She is taking a photograph of the Lord.' It sounded odd.

After *el Señor de la Vida* returned to the church I went and bought my breakfast (it was after twelve) off a sweet barrow standing in the plaza—delicious almond toffee which I got the man to break up with a hammer. Treated the nearby children to a lollipop apiece which soon cleared the barrow—and the owner was delighted with his fiesta sales. Lunched very early at 2.30 p.m. off the familiar saffron-coloured garlic-flavoured broth with bits of bread floating in it followed by a stew of chick-peas, potatoes and pork bones with a little meat adhering to them, and slices of black pudding.

This being a fiesta in Belmez it was a whole holiday for everyone and at 4 p.m. there was a clay pigeon shooting competition on a little green hill outside the *pueblo*. I rode over and watched this for a bit and every competitor split every plate which the catapult hurtled into the air before him so I cannot imagine who won. Stayed twenty minutes then returned through the village in an attempt to ride up to the Moorish fort behind it. This proved quite impossible and I was more than ever convinced that these fortresses and watch-towers, these Castles in Spain, exist only in our imaginations: that an invisible giant with a mania for landscape gardening moves them about in the night for fun. No castle ever seems to be in the same place two days running and if you try to ride or walk up to one, or to the even more elusive solitary watch-tower, you will inevitably find it is not there. But return to where you started from and there it is again, looking provokingly down from its precarious perch. I am not going to chase them any more. Except for the solid castle surrounded by houses in a *pueblo* from which they cannot escape (as at Jódar) they always beat me in the disappearing game.

Riding home I watched the sun setting on the sierras which had looked so gloomy and wet two nights before when I rode down into the valley of the Jandula off the rain-sodden *Sierra de la Cruz*. I reflected that only thirty kilometres away lay the paradisiacal infernal regions of Don Diego with little Juan Jesús wailing in the *posada*, an unknown donor's blood coursing through his tiny veins; and Doña Encarna teaching the beautiful troglodyte girls at their little blue desks, and the young *cura* working away at the dialogue Mass; I had ridden round an elliptical course and in two days would be back where I started from.

That evening I went along to the *párroco's* house next to the church to help him with his English. His two sisters lived with him and did the housekeeping. He was sitting at his desk when I entered and his sisters kept coming in and out, so did several men who were presented to me. This coming and going is a characteristic feature of life in the *pueblos* both in the peasant and professional classes. No one seems to remain alone for long: neighbours are always popping in and out or you are popping in to them for a gossip at the cosy-table. For this reason, as I have already said, I craved to be alone on my cross-country rides, the better to prepare myself for the hectic social life of the *pueblos*.

An English lesson

Don Alberto played me part of one of his English language records and it was very odd to hear English spoken very slowly and clearly and uncolloquially and all in the present tense in this remote mountain village. I suggested a little conversation practice but this was not very successful because he was at the same stage as I was at the beginning of my tour when I could only recite sentences I had learned by heart and could never understand what people said in reply. I tried to lead the conversation into church channels. . . .

Me: 'Your sermon was very good this morning.'
Don Alberto: 'Here is your friend John with his bicycle.'
Me: 'What time is Rosary to-night?'
Don Alberto: 'Have you any roses? We have no roses but we have some tulips.'
Me (becoming exasperated): 'Is that a photograph of your Bishop?' (Pointing to the wall) 'IS THAT A PHOTOGRAPH OF YOUR BISHOP?'
Don Alberto (without raising his eyes from his grammar book): 'She is not well, her appetite is not good.'

It was time for evening devotions. I asked what time Mass would be in the morning. Don Alberto asked when I would like it. Said I would be most grateful if he would say it at 7.30 a.m. as I wanted to make an early start for la Fuensanta.

Back in the *posada* I found an old gypsy woman with her beautiful daughter. They had come up by 'bus from Huelma to sell the baskets they had made. These were stacked at the end of the living-room beside the chemical spray man's scooter. We all sat round the cosy-table. I wanted to mend the lining of my coat, but found it impossible to thread a needle in such a dim light even with my spectacles on. The old gypsy woman threaded it for me without any spectacles. She said she would be grateful for an overcoat if I had one I did not use any more. Had I been St Martin I would have taken out my *navaja* and cut mine in half on the spot. But I haven't got as far as that yet so I said I was very sorry but that this was the only coat I had brought to Spain with me and that I badly needed it for riding over the sierras. We talked of Fuensanta, and the chemical spray man said that he often visited the shrine on his scooter and had received many favours from *la Virgen tan milagrosa de Fuensanta*. He said the words *tan milagrosa* (so miraculous) in such a caressing tone that one could feel his love for the Virgin mother of God. Then he told me the story of la Fuensanta, the sacred spring. . . . 'A Moorish Queen of Granada turned Christian, which so annoyed her husband that he cut off her right hand. She prayed to Our Lady who told her to bathe the stump in a certain spring which she did, and her hand was restored.'

I did some writing till supper at 11 p.m. which consisted of fried eggs and chips, bread, and custard apples. While we were eating, the gypsies left the cosy-table and went and sat by the fire. Downstairs *posada* guests generally feed themselves. Later, when the old gypsy disappeared into the depths of the stable to relieve nature, her daughter kept guard at the door. I had no one to keep guard for me. I used to try to hide behind the Marquesa.

The gypsies put down straw palliasses on the cold stone floor with an icy draught blowing under the front door and settled down, apparently happily, for the night. I got guilt as I went up to bed when I thought of this old woman and her daughter, the mother of three young children, sleeping in such discomfort while I retired to rather a damp bed with a mattress full of walnuts. Guilt was slightly relieved when I fell as usual headlong down the stone step into my bedroom and sprained my wrist on the rough stone floor.

Living outside time

FRIDAY, DECEMBER I

Mass started only five minutes late. I gave the Marquesa a good feed before I went to church but could not get a good feed myself when I came back. The café was shut and the *posada* fire was out, so I drank a glass of icy water and chewed a piece of dry bread as I packed my saddle-bags.

For the past month I had been living outside time. I was never late for anything because Mass and breakfast and luncheon and supper were always later than I was. Often I had ended up at quite a different place in the evening to the one I had settled for that morning. But it did not worry me at all. I just pottered about from *pueblo* to *pueblo* for pure pleasure. It had never been my intention to set up long-distance records and only once did our day's ride resemble an endurance test: that from Cazorla to Ubeda. I had not read a newspaper or used the telephone or spoken to anyone but Spaniards. I had got right back into the world of George Borrow and Richard Ford, for apart from the wireless and the naked 15-watt electric light bulb, rural Spain still remains exactly as they describe her. Now I suddenly realised that I had to return to the modern world inside time where there were such things as definite dates, and that I had an aeroplane to catch in Gibraltar in a few days from now so that I could not risk getting lost in any more sierras. For this reason I engaged my landlord, Diego Guz Gomez, to escort me to the shrine of Fuensanta on his donkey.

We set off a little before 9 a.m. which was the time of the sunrise, as we were just entering into December. There was such a maze of paths dividing and subdividing in all directions that even my guide got confused and had to ask the way at various farms we rode past. One muleteer we met said it was a *'camin muy malo'* (a phrase that was music in my ears) and that we had much better go by

139

the road: but that was a far longer way round and luckily Diego was as determined as I was to stick to the tracks. As usual the *camin muy malo* led us through country of such beauty that I longed for this beastly time which I was being forced back into to melt into eternity. The deep blue cloudless sky made the bad weather of the past fortnight seem like a half-forgotten dream. We had to cross a gully with a mountain torrent tumbling through it, then the track led up above the plough level to where the rocks were tinkling with sheep bells. I thought out a new riddle: What kind of animals have second sight?*

I never went out of a walk, so that the little white donkey could keep up with the mare. Noticed that she was shod in front but not behind and Diego told me that all donkeys are shod in this way whereas mules and horses are usually shod all round. Twice during our journey he patted her on the neck and said: '*¡Muy buena la burra!*' I asked if he fed her any barley but he said he could not afford to: she lived on *paja* and occasional grazing on which she appeared very fit. Diego told me the life of a *posada* keeper brought in very little cash. Most of the guests only wanted sleeping room on the floor and brought their own food with them. I had noticed that none of the smaller inns have bars or sell drinks.

At eleven o'clock Diego unexpectedly leapt from his donkey and produced a loaf of bread and some raw ham which we sat on a bank and ate with our *navajas* and some milk chocolate I found in a pocket of my jodhpurs. My inside was now in a very odd state owing to a chill I had caught on the Sierra de la Cruz. The raw ham tasted excellent but gave me a violent pain.

On we rode and reached the shrine after two and three-quarter hours' riding instead of the three and a half which Diego had told me it would take from Belmez.

* Answer: Spanish sheep because they see grass which is invisible to the naked human eye.

Huelma

The church at Fuensanta is built onto a big farmhouse in which several families live and work the surrounding land. One of the men took me to see the sacred spring out at the back which had restored the hand of the Queen of Granada. The church is larger than the one at Cuadro but about the same period, early seventeenth-century, white-washed within and without with no decoration. There is a very good Neapolitan crib in a glass case in the north aisle but ruined by out of scale modern plaster figures of the Holy Family. High above the altar stands a stiff little Virgin with a doll-like face wearing the usual rich brocade dress. I have been told that this dressing up of statues in real clothes rang the death knell of Spanish religious sculpture.

I said goodbye to Diego Gus Gomez and his *buena burra blanca* and proceeded on the mare to Huelma while they returned to Belmez. A good broad track below the shrine of the Fuensanta leads through olive groves to an unmetalled road which winds downhill for four kilometres into Huelma. Above this *pueblo* sits the best preserved twin-towered toy fortress I have ever seen. Had decided to remain here only for lunch and to reach Montejicar by nightfall, but as so often happened, God planned otherwise.

The *posada* was in the central plaza and I tied the Marquesa up in the roomy stable at the back, bought her some *cebada* in a nearby grocer's and told the landlord I would only leave her for a couple of hours. I went myself to an excellent large café on the other side of the plaza which was the Fortnum and Mason of Huelma with all sorts of tinned and bottled delicacies and wines and liquors stacked on shelves along the walls and a variety of *tapas* (snacks) on plates along the counter. Decided to lunch off these and got myself a boat-shaped plate of tunny fish, tomatoes, and baby artichokes, and a bottle of Citrania, my favourite lemonade.

141

While I was drinking coffee at the end of my meal a wiry little man of about sixty came up to my table, bowed, said good afternoon and drew a slip of paper from his breast pocket and handed it to me. On it were written the words: 'Penelope Valentine Hester Chetwode. Born 14th February 1910'.

I said: 'But Señor, where did you get this information?'

'We met at Don Alberto's last night!' he replied. He had obviously been one of the men who had dropped into the parish priest's house during the English lesson.

'And you must have got my name and date of birth from the Civil Guard?'

He smiled and insisted on taking me to his house for lunch. I protested that I had just had it but could not explain that my inside was in a state of volcanic eruption. He lived in a very well-appointed two-storey house just below the *posada* with a large garage and a walled garden at the back. The living-rooms were all on the first floor and included a modern bathroom and W.C. We had luncheon at a cosy-table by the window: very good chicken broth, fried octopus, raw home-cured ham, grapes and pomegranates. Over the broth I lamented the fact that the wireless had replaced the guitar in every *posada*: that all the English nineteenth-century travellers wrote that a guitarist was never wanting and that he accompanied singers and dancers every evening. The son-in-law of the house, Don Juan de Dios Guzman Justicia, said they had a mad old labourer who played *flamenco* very well by ear as he could neither read a note of music nor a word of literature. Within ten minutes the old boy was seated in the sitting-room on a chair close to the cosy-table, his long lean unshaven Iberian features transfixed by the beauty of the Sevillianas and fandangoes he was playing.

The household consisted of the mother and father, their daughter and son-in-law and their three little boys, all living amicably in the same house with three maids to look after them including a fat, pretty, happy thirteen-year-old girl whose chief duty appeared to be to wait at table and play with the children. Was she really being deprived through not remaining at school? We make such a fuss about education and spend so much money on secondary modern schools yet many of the older pupils in them still cannot read and write properly. And will our girls make such efficient and therefore contented wives and mothers as their Spanish counterparts who to-day can not only read and write (I tested several of them) but have a good knowledge of Christian doctrine and can sew and wash and iron quite beautifully?

My friends owned three farms in the locality including one near Belmez which is why I met the grandfather, Don Juan Jerez Dias, at Don Alberto's house. They do most of their field work with mule teams and told me that each animal gets an allowance of three kilos of barley a day, just on seven pounds. I told them how pleased I was to see all the Andalusian mules in such splendid condition but could not understand why they were trace-clipped upside down leaving the loins bare and the full winter coat on the belly. Nobody has been able to explain this any more than they know why a donkey mare has the tuft left on the end of her tail and a stallion has it clipped off. The answer is always the same: '¡Es costumbre!' (It is the custom.)

It was too late to think of riding on to another village so I went next door to the *posada* and told the landlord that I wanted a room for the night, then I changed into my one and only skirt which always came out of its old woollen stocking without a crease, and was taken along by the ladies of the Jerez household, mother and daughter, to see the large renaissance church which was very fine outside but over restored inside with no interesting works of art. The parish priest and his curate at Huelma are brothers and one of them was about to baptise an infant when we went in. I was invited to play the harmonium which I did extremely badly for ten minutes. The register was very stiff and the only music I could find that I knew was *Stille Nacht* and the *Missa de Angelis* which seems to be as popular in Spain as it is in England.

Just outside the west door of the church there was a splendid view of the toy fortress which I think was close enough to the town not to do a disappearing act had I tried to climb up to it.

We next went to see the Señora's old mother of eighty-seven who lived nearby and was stone deaf. She sat at her cosy-table crocheting with an unmarried daughter beside her who went off to confession when we arrived. As soon as she returned we had an Anglo-Spanish tea-party consisting of bread and *butter* (there being a herd of Friesians on the outskirts of Huelma which I had passed in the morning) and honey, coffee, and two plates of sliced salami, one black and one red.

The Señora and I then went to evening devotions when the harmonium was rather well played and the singing quite good. Afterwards she took me to the casino, the club above the excellent café, frequented by the professional men of the *pueblo*. We were the only women there and I felt very honoured, as if I had been asked into Whites. We sat down at a table and I drank two bottles of Citrania while speaking very slowly and clearly in English to two new pupils who were presented to me: the local doctor and the *Alcalde* (Mayor) who was also the headmaster of the boys' school. The latter had been in touch with the British Council in Madrid and was very keen on everything English. I told him truthfully that he spoke better than either the doctor or Don Alberto. We all three conversed for half an hour, the doctor being very pleased with: 'It rains cats and dogs', and he taught me the Spanish equivalent: '*lluvia a cantaros*'.* I remembered that a Spanish surgeon had been the first to do the operation of pre-frontal leucotomy and to explain this I drew a head on a piece of paper with a slice taken out of the top which was perfectly intelligible to him and in his own language he told me all about the Instituto de Investigaciónes Clínicas of the Madrid University.

SATURDAY, DECEMBER 2

I determined to have nothing but brandy and milk for my breakfast, in an attempt to settle my inside, so I went to the Fortnum Café where a woman was scrubbing the floor, and ordered it. The waiter brought me a glass of hot milk and a small glass of brandy which with a great effort I forced myself to drink and got temporary relief from my pain. It was extremely annoying to have at last succumbed to this interior complaint from which so many English suffer when they go to the south of Europe. Bought two apples in the market as I have great faith in their curative powers; then I went to say goodbye to my friends. It was 10.15 a.m. and they were just sitting down to breakfast of fried *churros* and coffee. Young Don Juan de Dios had broken his into a large bowl twice the size of a breakfast cup and poured his coffee on top of them and the oil in which they had been fried floated on top. The three little boys then ran in and showed me the pictures which I had inevitably drawn for them on the previous evening of St George and St James which they had coloured quite beautifully with their crayons. They all wanted to ride on the Marquesa, so when their father had finished his breakfast he helped me to lift them aboard, two on the saddle and one on the croup and walked them to the top of the *pueblo* where I

* *Cantaros* are the large earthenware jugs carried by donkeys to the communal water supply.

mounted and was directed onto a nice unmetalled country road leading out of a derelict little cobbled plaza. The Marquesa by this stage of the tour was answering so well to the aids that she struck off straight from a walk into a canter and I think we impressed the crowd of Huelmaites who had collected to witness our departure. But I never asked her to canter far in full battle array and when we slowed down to a walk (once out of sight of our admirers) I had to turn round every few minutes to revel in the beauty of Huelma Castle standing out against the backcloth of the deep blue Sierra de Magina over which I had ridden from shrine to shrine.

After an hour's riding, which I calculated to represent about seven kilometres, we went up to a white farmhouse on top of a hill and without any warning came upon the whole of the northern face of the now snow-covered Sierra Nevada running from east to west along the horizon. From now on for the last two days of the tour we were to ride through country dominated by the great range. Sometimes it would disappear altogether when we wound through gullies but it would always reappear a bit further on and delight us from some new angle: at least I speak for myself as the Marquesa thought of nothing but grass and acorns.

We got confused directions at the farm, or perhaps I did not listen to them very carefully, being stunned by the sudden appearance of the mountains, in any case we went at least three kilometres out of our way so I decided to retrace our steps as I could not afford the time to get completely lost any more. We had lunch by a tiny trickling stream with good grass. I ate my two badly bruised apples and then fell fast asleep in the sun, to awaken twenty minutes later with the Marquesa still grazing contentedly a hundred yards downstream. Eventually we reached Montejicar where I received excellent directions from a Civil Guard standing outside his barracks. I always called at these when possible as it is the business of the inmates to know every mule-track and goat-path in their area.

We rode westwards with the sun working round my left shoulder to set in my face. The track led over undulating farmland with the great mountains bounding the southern horizon. I do not think I have ever seen a more beautiful landscape, even in Kashmir. I rode along physically feeling the silence, my senses quickened by the knowledge that the tour was ending and my partnership with the stolid old Marquesa must be broken, perhaps for ever. I do not believe that she felt any real affection for me but I had gained her confidence: she knew she could depend on me for outsize feeds. She was often obstinate and had driven me silly because she would never go to a strange *fuente* without several minutes of patient coaxing; she would never allow herself to be led close enough up to a bank for me to mount with any ease (and there was not always a chair handy); but on the credit side she had proved wonderfully reliable, sure-footed and comfortable, could be trusted to graze without straying, and, through steady work and gluttony, was now in such splendid condition that I could hardly wait for Eudo and Rosemary to see her. Such muscle! Such a gloss on her bay coat! She looked as if she had had two hours' strapping a day but in point of fact the only grooming she got was to have the mud brushed off her legs and belly with the dandy brush. As for the feeding methods in southern Spain, I do not know how unboiled barley would answer for fast work (it is said to be bad for the wind), but for slow work it appears to be better than oats, or shall we say it brings more credit to the owner because of the wonderful gloss which it puts on the animal's coat.

Apart from the Marquesa's company which I had enjoyed during the past month, I had seen human beings as God meant them to be. Touring on a horse seems to bring out all the best in the characters of the people you meet and you do not see them for long enough to get on one another's nerves. The innkeepers and their wives and children, my fellow guests at the *posadas*, the families who put me up in their houses, the parish priests and their curates, even the much-abused members of the *Guardia Civil*, had all been out to help me; I had enjoyed only the most friendly and unselfish traits in their characters which, added to the extraordinary beauty of their countryside, made me feel that I had ridden through the garden of Paradise before the Fall.

Towards evening I got in a gully muddle. But a ploughman returning home with his mules put me right. He said that when I emerged at the further end I would see my destination, Campotejar, half-an-hour's ride away. I asked how long it would take me altogether and was horrified because I thought he said five hours. He actually said '*cinco cuartos*', five quarters, which was his way of saying an hour and a quarter. When we finally emerged from the gully there was a wide bridle road leading southwest, but no sign of a *pueblo*. As we went on into the gathering dusk to the sound of sheep bells I saw white smoke wreathing up from behind a little hill and I realised that Campotejar lay behind it. This white wood smoke is one of the many charms of Spanish *pueblos*, especially in the evenings and early mornings. And the smell varies with the district: barley straw, pine, olive, rosemary, lavender and marjoram according to what grows on the nearest hills or sierras. We were cantering along the soft earth track when I felt something jump out of my rucksack. It was my roll of lavatory-paper which had unwound itself for yards. I stopped to pick it up. A shepherd boy with a flock of sheep and goats was following but I am sure he did not know what it was and I therefore felt no embarrassment.

Evening ride into Campotejar

As we rode into Campotejar the bells were ringing for evening devotions but I was far too tired to think of anything but sleep. Eight hours' riding on an empty stomach proved better than the strongest sleeping pill. And in all that time I had not gone along one foot of tarmac and had only seen one car on the little road leading out of Huelma.

The *posada* was in a wide street of low houses and was the only one I struck on my tour in which there were separate entrances for the human beings and the beasts of burden. You had to walk right round to the back to reach the stable door where seven donkeys stood in a row munching *paja*. Fortunately my landlord had his own supply of *cebada* so I did not have to go out in search of a shop. I walked back into the house through a series of two or three store-rooms and across a tiny open yard in which there was a loo which once more displayed the profound originality of *posada* architects: it had four walls but no ceiling. You sat on the pan and looked straight up at the stars. Sir Edwin Lutyens had the same idea at New Delhi, but for a reception room in the Viceroy's House. Fortunately it was a fine night.

I was shown into a nice bedroom with a good leaning washstand, some pegs on the walls and an even stone floor on which I immediately spread my brown paper bedside mat. Having unpacked I went down to the little narrow kitchen which had no windows at all but a lovely wide fireplace with plenty of banked up smouldering *paja* providing a good heat. I sat on a low chair under the hood and ordered two boiled eggs for supper and fell fast asleep. At nine my landlady woke me and took me into a brightly lit dining-room with a really warm cosy-table. I ate one and a half eggs and fell asleep again on my crossed arms. At 10.15 I was woken up by a single member of the Civil Guard who wanted to establish my identity. I sadly recited my piece for the last time: 'I am

149

English, I am on a tour in these sierras, I come from the farm of the English Duke of Wellington and Ciudad Rodrigo . . .' As usual he spent more time poring over the Marquesa's papers than over mine.

SUNDAY, DECEMBER 3

I had never slept better throughout my tour, and fortunately woke at 6.30 a.m. so that I could go to the early Mass and get off in good time to reach Illora by nightfall.

Found the way to the church easily by the light of the waning moon and the women walking towards it. A small plain building with my ideal retablo: a huge crucifix on the whitewashed wall behind the altar. Redecoration was in progress so that all the statues had been shoved into a side chapel. The church was very full but only about thirty per cent were men. The *cura's* little sleek black terrier sat near the west door. As I was returning from the altar somebody trod on it and the poor little animal let out a piercing yelp.

I went to the café bang next door to the *posada* for breakfast and had two large glasses of white coffee and some stale biscuits. No *tortas* available. A man sitting at the next table had a little mongrel which he told me never left him and was more intelligent than a lot of men he knew. '*¡Solo le falta hablar!*' he said, while he fondled it as lovingly as any English dog-lover.

We managed to get off by 9 a.m. and left the village in a sun-soaked mist with bells ringing through it for the second Mass. An unmetalled road led onto a metalled one along which I had to ride for a few kilometres on my way to Benalua. I heard the sound of cantering hooves behind me and turned round and saw a man on a thirteen-hand bay pony. He caught up with me and said he had heard as he left Campotejar that I was riding alone to Benalua and thought I might like company. I could not say what I felt: 'Oh God how can I make conversation to you for an hour and a half? I would much rather ride alone!' However he turned out to be such a nice man that in the end I was glad to ride with him. His name was Juan Santiago and he lived in the *calle de la Virgen* with his wife to whom he had been married for a year and was rather worried because no baby had appeared. He owned this one pony called Gamba (Prawn), a twelve-year-old mare like the Marquesa, and he earned his living by selling wine round the district, but now he was going to Benalua to fetch some sacks of flour from the mill. We proceeded to trot in single file along the unmetalled verge of the road, but after a couple of kilometres he shouted out: '¡*Gamba se cansa!*' (Gamba is tiring). So I pulled back into a walk for the remainder of the journey. No English horse-lover could have been more considerate for his animal than this Spanish pedlar. He told me she was a very good pony and he patted her neck several times saying: '¡*Muy buena Gamba!*' Then he got onto the subject of olive oil and asked if we had much of it in England. I said no but that we had butter instead, but that our bread was not nearly so good as Spanish bread. Juan said he would not like to come to England. He could not imagine living without olive oil and good bread, and look at all the splendid products of the pig which his countrymen enjoyed! I said we also had pigs and was on the point of extolling the excellence of roast lamb and mint sauce, roast beef and Yorkshire pudding, but apart from the fact that I could not translate the latter I thought it immoral to disturb his contentment. Eventually we got to Benalua and parted company.

I was now back on my tracks and rode ten kilometres through the same winding valley to Colomera as I had done in reverse direction on my outward journey. This was the only stretch of road I duplicated in a month.

Emerging at the far end the Marquesa and I were once more confronted with the great range of the Sierra Nevada which daily grew larger as we got closer to it. We turned off along a bridle road to the west and I was delighted to see a smallholder and his family all eating their lunch under an olive tree and making the most of the sunny December day. We exchanged greetings and remarks on the loveliness of the landscape. Further along the track we saw, high up on a grey sierra to our right, the most dramatically castle-crowned crag of the whole tour. It suddenly dawned on me that this was Moclín where I had stayed the first night with Eugenia and Fernando. I still had a few of the delicious milky almonds which she had given me.

We came to Los Olivares, the straggling village at the foot of the precipice below Moclín. Our stony track divided and I asked a young man sitting on a low wall the best one to take but he and his (twin?) brother stared vacantly at me and I realised they were idiots. How much happier they must be living here in familiar surroundings than in a loony bin.

I muddled my way along by the sun and the sierras towards Illora through a smoky little *pueblo* called Tiena la Baja from which a broad earth track led across ploughed fields to the main Cordoba–Granada road. I saw the rock path to the north leading up the little sierra towards Moclín where I had dismounted and slid under the Marquesa on the first day out, and reflected that had she inadvertently trodden on my head instead of on my leg on that occasion my tour would have ended abruptly there and then. Across the main road I found a short cut through the olive groves which led down to the un-metalled Illora road. We reached the *pueblo* at five o'clock and were greeted by a touching young man who was dumb but who recognised the Marquesa and barked with joy and followed us making the most extraordinary noises, indicating the complicated cross-country route to La Torre. The Marquesa appeared to know where she was so I threw the reins at her but she took me to the mule stud at the farm instead of to the Duke's house two kilometres above it. So true to form we had gone the wrong way to the last. At least we landed in the wrong place from my point of view but the Marquesa did not think so and I had a bit of difficulty in urging her up the hill away from the familiar barn to the grand stables where a huge loose-box awaited her.

Returning a borrowed horse to a southern Irishman and an Andalusian groom was a pretty tall order as a more horsey combination could hardly be met with. But conscious of the Marquesa's rippling muscles and glossy coat I was full of self-confidence as I rode her into the yard which was justified by Eudo's complimentary remarks and the groom's ear-to-ear grin.

The next morning I went to say goodbye to my companion, the other middle-aged lady. She was standing knee-deep in long wheat straw, eating as usual. I went up to pat her but when she saw I brought no *cebada* she laid back her ears, presented her quarters and pulled some more luscious lucerne hay out of the rack. Perhaps St Thomas is right. Can I really love her when so obviously she does not love me back?